Let's face

You frequently shoot (

You don't have a handicap, but think you know it.

You are always on the lookout for a good deal on greens fees.

You have a garage full of clubs that didn't feel or look right.

You think that *Golf Magazine®* and *Golf Digest®* are filled with too much hype on equipment and courses you can't afford.

You won't buy that cool driver until it's on sale.

You watch the *Golf Channel®* for tips on how to play better.

You have unused training aids that sit in your closet.

You plan a golf trip and play more golf in a week than you play the rest of the year.

You lose a lot of golf balls, but still try to hit miracle shots.

You think a good day on the golf course is when you end the day with more golf balls than when you started.

Every time ***you*** tee off you think that this round will be your best.

One day ***your*** putting is the best part of your game, then your driver, then nothing.

You worry about playing a new course because you don't have any information on it except hype, reputation and difficulty.

You play some courses only because you've got a coupon.

You risk playing new courses only because your friends told you to.

You think that existing golf course guides don't tell you anything.

You have found a guide that understands your game...

HACKER'S GUIDE™

Real Ratings by Real People!™

to Twin Cities Golf Courses

The Complete Ratings Guide for
All 18-Hole Public Golf Courses in the Twin Cities

Publisher & Production Supervisor
Bruce D. Stasch, the Ultimate Hacker

Published and distributed by
Apex Golf Enterprises a division of
Apex Mountain Holdings Corporation
4317 Washburn Avenue North
Minneapolis, MN 55412
877-939-0458
inquiries@hackersguides.com
www.hackersguides.com

Acknowledgements

A guide like this cannot be completed by one person. It took *Team Hacker*, a group of enthusiastic and dedicated golfers that personally visited every course listed in this book. Without this group, the book would never have gotten finished. *Team Hacker* members included:

Adam Johnson *(St. Paul)*; Al Cooper *(Albertville)*; Andrew Jackola *(North St. Paul)*; Brett Mueller *(St. Paul)*; Dave Buzza *(Minneapolis)*; Dave Prehal *(Eagan)*; Dennis Delmont *(Maplewood)*; Duncan Ryhorchuk *(Hanover)*; Glen Roseen *(Wyoming)*; Jay Rasmussen *(Minneapolis)*; Jesse Zeien *(New Brighton)*; Jordan Osterman *(New Hope)*; Justin Rice *(Minneapolis)*; Kenneth Willwert, Jr. *(St. Paul)*; Kimberly Stasch *(Cold Spring)*; Mark Johnson *(Lake Elmo)*; Pat Barrett *(Lake Elmo)*; and Rex Schmidt *(Bloomington)*.

Also, many others helped during the production of this book; from my attorney to my printer, distributor, designer and illustrator. Without these folks, the idea of rating every public golf course in the Twin Cities would have never happened. In addition, four sets of eyes are better than one so to my proofreaders, Sara Fisher, Eve Sotnak, and Dawn Carlstrom, thank you for correcting my mistakes.

Finally, I'd like to dedicate this book to my parents Marcia and Jesse Stasch who always believed that once I set my mind to something, it could get done. Also, thanks to my wife, Eve, for allowing me to play way too much golf and being willing to become a golf widow for most of the summer.

HACKER'S GUIDE™

Real Ratings by Real People!™

to Twin Cities Golf Courses

The Complete Ratings Guide for
All 18-Hole Public Golf Courses in the Twin Cities

The reviews published in this guide are based on public opinion surveys, with numerical ratings reflecting the average scores given by all reviewers assigned to a particular course. The same scoring system has been used by all reviewers and the values and write-ups are solely the opinion of the reviewers. Course data including phone numbers, addresses, distances and other factual information were correct to the best of our knowledge when this guide was published. The publisher cannot accept responsibility for facts that have become outdated or for errors or omissions. For the most accurate information, please consult a course's website or contact the course directly, especially if you are planning on visiting it soon.

No portion of this book may be reproduced in any form without the written permission from the publishers.

Cover Design & Illustrations by Kevin Cannon and Zander Cannon

© 2008-2009 Apex Golf Enterprises
The Hacker's Guide to Golf™ is a registered
trademark of Apex Golf Enterprises a division of
Apex Mountain Holdings Corporation
ISBN-13: 978-0-615-23465-6
ISBN-10: 0-615-23465-8
Printed in the United States of America

Table of Contents

Why do you need this book?

Let's face it. Most of us do not play golf well enough to ever join a professional golf tour. If fact, a professional golfer probably plays more golf in a week than we get to play all summer. With so little time and even less money, we don't want to waste the few chances we get by playing a course where the staff is rude, the food stinks, the course is too hard and we paid way too much for what we got.

As golfers, we tend to play it safe and are reluctant to try new golf courses. We don't want to drive clear across town to end up playing a bad course and have an awful experience. Sometimes, we turn to guidebooks or recommendations from friends, but they all seem to have played the same course and every guidebook review says the same thing.

We decided to do something about it and created a golf course guide that looks at the entire golf experience—hospitality, playability, usability, facility and value—not just the beauty of a golf course.

Welcome to the *Hacker's Guide to Twin Cities Golf Courses*, a complete rating and review of every 18-hole public golf course in the 11-county Metro area. Yes, that's right. Every public golf course from St. Francis to Lakeville, Buffalo to Hastings. Public, semi-private, resort and executive eighteens. They have all been personally reviewed and played by a member of *Team Hacker*—real golfers rating real golf courses.

We hope you enjoy our new book and if you like this one, you're going to want to buy our future guides, too. We'd love to hear what you think so send us an e-mail.

Bruce D. Stasch
Publisher
ultimatehacker@hackersguides.com

1

Why do we call them Hacker's Guides?

National Golf Foundation (NGF) research shows that <u>only 22% of all golfers regularly score better than 90 for 18 holes</u> on a regulation length course. For females, the percentage is just 7% and for males it is 25%. The average 18-hole score on a full-size course is 97 for men and 114 for women. It's an even 100 for all golfers. Only 6% of the men and 1% of the women say they break 80 regularly. When asked what they'd like to shoot, most golfers say they'd be satisfied if they could shoot 85 on an 18-hole regulation course on a regular basis. The average scores have changed very little over the years. With these statistics in mind, we are targeting the <u>78% of the golfing public that are hackers</u>. All of the golf magazines and golf guides on the market target the hard-core, highly active and economically well-off golfer, but that group only represents 22% of the market. The *Hacker's Guides* are real course ratings for real people.

How does our Hacker Rating System work?

The goal of the *Hacker Rating System* is to assess a course on its friendliness to an average golfer, not a pro. So a *Hacker's Guide* rating might be different than other guides and some favorite courses might have a rating that is different than what you'd expect. The rating system analyzes a golf course on forty different factors in five different categories. These categories each have a value that adds up to a maximum rating of 1000 points. The rating categories are broken out into

five distinct areas: Hospitality (25%) = 250 points, Playability (30%) = 300 points, Usability (20%) = 200 points, Facility (15%) = 150 points and Value (10%) = 100 points. Each rating category is then broken into 8-10 areas that are assessments of specific factors. The formula that was used to come up with a final rating is proprietary.

The Hacker Rating System

The *Hacker Rating System* is a scoring system that looks at a golf course from the perspective of the "hacker" or modestly skilled player. It takes into account both on- and off-course factors when coming up with an overall rating. Each of the 40 factors that make up the scoring are weighted within each category (for example 8.25 out of 10) and each category makes up a certain percentage of the total score. A perfect score in all categories would be 1000 points.

Independent raters from *Team Hacker* visited each course during the summer/fall of 2008. They played each course, talked to the management, drove the cart, toured the facility, ate in the restaurant or bar, warmed up on the putting green and practiced hitting golf balls on the range. They did not ask for or receive any special treatment so that they could experience the golf course from the perspective of an average customer. Some of the factors that were considered:

Hospitality (25%) = 250 points

Professionalism. Friendliness of staff and guests. Does the beverage cart appear often? Check-in. Does the course reach out to women? Pace-of-play. How friendly were the natives? Quality of the food and food service.

Playability (30%) = 300 points

Is this course suitable for a 20+ handicap golfer? Course conditions - cart paths, fairways, tees & greens. Lots of hazards? Safe outs for average players. Hilly or can you walk?

Usability (20%) = 200 points

Signage easy to understand? Flow from hole to hole and from the course to the clubhouse. What about the website? Online tee times. Getting to the first tee?

Facility (15%) = 150 points

Overall conditions of the clubhouse, driving range, putting area and parking lot? The bar and restaurant. Walkable? Short distances between holes. What is missing?

Value (10%) = 100 points

Did you get your money's worth? Cart rental prices. Food. What about memberships? Deals and specials. Would you come back?

Who is Team Hacker?

Every one of the golf courses in the *Hacker's Guide* will have been personally rated by a member of *Team Hacker*. *Team Hacker* members come from the ranks of teachers, seniors, writers, students; real golfers rating real courses. A member will typically have an average handicap of 80-110 for men and 95-125 for women.

This team has personally visited each golf course, met with course management, answered an extensive list of assessment questions and played the golf course just like any other golfer. They did not request any special VIP treatment from the course while they were there. In addition to the course rating, each course in this guide has also been given a 400-word review based on that team member's personal playing experience. No other golf course directory or rating guide exists that spends as much time assessing a course in this manner.

How can I become a member of Team Hacker?

Team Hacker members are not paid to provide golf course ratings. They are just a group of men and women that enjoy golf and are willing to provide their opinions to the millions of fellow golfers out there. They don't do this for a living, don't work for a golf course that they rated, and feel that their opinions will help others decide what golf course to play.

What are the perks?

Although you can't make a living rating golf courses for *Team Hacker* (wouldn't that be nice?) there are a few perks. The biggest is being able to play golf courses for free or at a big discount. Also, you'll receive *Team Hacker* gear and chances to win free golf trips.

Anyone is eligible to become a member of *Team Hacker*. All they need to do is visit our website **www.hackersguides.com** and fill out the registration form. We will contact you when we add to our team.

Why this guide is different

Existing rating books and systems only seem to look at the golf course's difficulty and fail to consider other factors that affect having an enjoyable golfing experience. Scores are arbitrary and most books don't even know who is actually making the rating. For all we know it could be the golf pro rating his own course. For 95% of men and 99% of women, breaking 80 is a rarity and shooting par will only be a dream. So playing the famous courses that the professionals do will only frustrate us. This guide is for the rest of us that are defined as hackers (you know who you are).

By creating this book, we wanted to dig deeper and look at a broader range of factors that make up the golfing experience and we wanted the same people who rated the courses to be the same people that would read our book. Hackers should know what hackers want from a golf course.

How to use this book

Keep it in your car or golf bag. Use it as your golf travel planner. Play the Top Ten in one of the rating categories. If you are a beginner, look for courses that provide the right amount of challenge for your game. If you play a lot of golf, look for a better golfing experience, not just a better golf course. Hey, if it is a nice sunny day and you just drove past a course you never heard of, pull out the book and see if it is worth playing. When you're done, tell us about it at **www.hackersguides.com**.

What about those cool icons?

Every so often you will see icons that appear on some of the pages in this book. All of them have something to do with Minnesota. It could be a tidbit on a Minnesota-born golfer, unique facts about Minnesota golf, famous Minnesota golfing events, historic details about Minnesota courses and the tournaments held there, or a host of other Minnesota golf facts. Look for them.

How do I read a Hacker Review?

1 Course Details: Includes basic contact info, type of course (public, semi-private), par and website.

4 Region: For this guide, all courses are in the Twin Cities Region. Margin tabs also subdivide the Twin Cities Region into Northwest, Northeast, Southwest and Southeast sections.

BOULDER POINTE

Region: Twin Cities

9575 Glenborough Drive
Elko, MN 55020
Clubhouse: 952-461-4900
Golf Shop: 952-461-4900
Type: Public   Par: 71
www.boulderpointegolf.com

Course Rating

HOSPITALITY	6.12
PLAYABILITY	7.50
USABIL	7.35
FACILIT	7.01
VALUE	6.15

OVERALL SCORE
692

Tees	Men's	Women's	Yards
Red	64.7/118	69.0/122	4794
Gold	67.6/123	72.5/129	5426
White	69.5/126		5833
Black	71.2/131		6224

Greens Fee: $34.00 (weekend)
1/2 Cart Fee: $15.00 (weekend)

2 Scoring Details: Includes tee boxes for men and women, par rating, slope rating and yardages. Some tee box options for courses with more than 18 holes may have been excluded because of space.

3 Favorite Icon: If a course has ranked in the Top Ten in any category or in overall score, they have received a *Hacker's Favorite Award*.

5 Course Ratings: Weighted scores based on how 40 different questions were answered by a course rater. Each category score is based on a total of 10 points (e.g., 6.35 out of 10).

6 Overall Score: Courses score a maximum total of 1000 points. This score is based on the weighting of the five categories.

7 Fees: Obtained from each course's website weekend fees information and were current as of October 2008.

Minnesota's Golf Obsession

How many golfers are there in the U.S.?
There are 29.5 million golfers in the United States.[1] A golfer is defined as a person that has played at least one round in the last year. More importantly, there are 17.3 million "core" golfers (those that golf at least 8 times/year). The *National Golf Foundation* (NGF) estimates that there are 500 million rounds of golf played annually in the United States.

How many golf courses are there in the U.S.?
There are approximately 16,000 courses in the United States. The top five states for golf are Florida, South Carolina, North Carolina, California and Arizona (Minnesota ranks #11 in the total number of courses).

How many golfers are there in Minnesota?
The State of Minnesota has a population of 5.19 million people[2] and often ranks 1st or 2nd in the country with the highest level of participation by its residents. Minnesota has 733,000 golfers which represent 2.9% of the U.S. golf population.

How many "core" golfers are there in Minnesota?
Of the 733,000 Minnesota golfers, the core Minnesota golfers represent 11.8% of the total or 87,000 golfers. These golfers play an average of 20+ rounds annually.

How many golf courses are in Minnesota?
According to the Minnesota Golf Association[3], Minnesota has 508 golf courses in the state: 55 private, 351 public/daily fee, 83 municipal, and 19 resort, with nearly 90 percent of Minnesota golf courses open to the public (457 courses).

[1]National statistics are from 2007 and were provided by the *National Golf Foundation*.
[2]State population is based on 2007 *U.S. Census Bureau* estimate.
[3]State golf course data is based on 2008 *Minnesota Golf Association* statistics.

A Few Famous Minnesota Golfers

Tim Herron (born 2/6/70 in Minneapolis)
Was nicknamed "Lumpy" during his first day on the job at a
golf course in Wayzata, Minnesota. His grandfather, Carson
Lee Herron, played in the 1934 U.S. Open and won state titles
in Minnesota and Iowa. His father, also named Carson, played
in the 1963 U.S. Open. Sister Alissa won the 1999 U.S. Mid-Am-
ateur and is a three-time Minnesota Amateur champion. Won
over $15.7 million in his career. Went to the University of New
Mexico. Has won four tournaments on the PGA Tour. Currently
lives in Deephaven, Minnesota. Turned pro in 1993.

Tom Lehman (born 3/7/59 in Austin, Minnesota)
Born in Austin and grew up in Alexandria. He was a three-time
NCAA All-American with the Gophers in 1979, 1980 and 1981.
He won the 1996 British Open and was named PGA Player of
the Year the same season. His golf course design firm, Lehman
Design Group, has worked on the Somerby Golf Club in Byron,
Minnesota; the TPC Twin Cities in Blaine (site of the 3M Cham-
pionship on the Champions Tour); and The Gallery Golf Club
in Tucson, Arizona. He has career earnings of $20.3 million on
the PGA. Has won five tournaments on the PGA Tour & four on
the Nationwide Tour. His brother, Jim Lehman, Jr., is his agent.
Turned pro in 1982.

John Harris (born 6/13/52 in Minneapolis)
Created the Harris-Homeyer Insurance Company in 1979 with
Bill Homeyer, father of former U.S. Women's Open champion,
Hilary Lunke. Attended the University of Minnesota on a
hockey scholarship, but also played golf, earning first team
All-America honors in golf in 1974. Played for Herb Brooks at
the University of Minnesota and was the second leading scorer
for the 1974 team that won the NCAA Championship. Grew up
playing a nine-hole course with sand greens in northern Minnesota. Turned pro in 1976 and again in 2002.

A Few Famous Minnesota Golfers

Patty Berg (born 1918 in Minneapolis, died 9/10/06)
Berg took up golf when she was 13. In 1934, aged 16, she won the Minneapolis City Championship. That was the first of 29 victories during an illustrious amateur career. She won her first Major, the Titleholders, in 1937. She played in the Curtis Cup in 1936 and 1938. When war broke out in 1942, she joined the navy and served as a lieutenant in the Marine Corps until 1945. After the war, she helped to set up the LPGA in 1948 and became its first president. Berg won 57 tournaments on the LPGA Tour. The LPGA honored her by establishing the Patty Berg Award in 1978 which is given to the lady golfer who has made the greatest contribution to women's golf during the year. Turned pro in 1940.

Hilary Lunke (born Hilary Homeyer 6/7/79 in Edina)
On July 7, 2003, Lunke defeated Kelly Robbins and Angela Stanford in an 18-hole playoff to win the U.S. Women's Open for her first, and so far only, LPGA win. Lunke was also the first player to win the U.S. Open after advancing through local and sectional qualifying. Lunke's husband, Tylar, was her caddie on that July day. They married on November 2, 2002. Lunke gave birth to her first child, Greta Elin, in November of 2007. Attended Stanford University. Turned pro in 2002.

Lee Janzen (born 8/28/64 in Austin, Minnesota)
Born in Minnesota, but spent most of his childhood in Baltimore, Maryland and then moved to Florida when he was twelve. Won his first amateur tournament when he was fifteen, attended Florida Southern University and was part of the team that won the Division II National Championships in 1985 and 1986. Has won eight times on the PGA Tour, most notably the U.S. Open in 1993 and 1998. He's played on two Ryder Cup teams (1993 & 1997). He has also won the Players Championship in 1995. Won over $14.3 million in his career. Turned pro in 1986.

NOTE: This is a very small sample of the many Minnesotans that have been involved in the world of golf. More stories will be found in future *Hacker's Guides*.

2009 Hacker's Favorite Course Award

Since the *Hacker's Guide* is so particular in what it determines is a good golfing experience, we wanted to acknowledge golf courses that, according to our *Team Hacker* raters, represent the best the area has to offer. The *Hacker's Favorite Course Award* is awarded to those courses that scored in the Top Ten for any of the five rating categories (Hospitality, Playability, Usability, Facility & Value) as well as the Top Ten courses in Overall Score. Some courses may find themselves award winners in more than one category. Each course will have received a certificate suitable for framing and hopefully are displaying that award in a prominent place in the golf shop.

On the next two pages you will see who finished in the top ten in each category and on each course review is listed what category(s) the course was awarded a *2009 Hacker's Favorite Course Award*.

H — Hospitality **F** — Facility

P — Playability **V** — Value

U — Usability

Congratulations to all the winners!

Hacker's Favorite Winners

TOP TEN

TOTAL SCORE (out of 1000 points)

The Refuge	883	Chaska Town	866
River Oaks	873	The Links at Northfork	863
Deer Run	871	Wild Marsh	854
Braemar	869	Applewood Hills	854
Elk River	866	Bunker Hills	847

NOTE: *Thirty-one different courses received a Hacker's Favorite Course Award in 2009. Some more than one.*

HOSPITALITY (out of 10 points)

Ridges at Sand Creek	9.52	Gem Lake Hills	9.28
Applewood Hills	9.45	Hidden Haven	9.25
Deer Run	9.38	River Oaks	9.24
Eagle Valley	9.32	Chaska Town	9.08
Braemar	9.31	Majestic Oaks (Signature)	9.05

NOTE: *The category in which a golf course generally had its highest score was Hospitality and the lowest was Value. Does that mean the cheaper the course the nicer the people?*

PLAYABILITY (out of 10 points)

Elk River	9.20	Chaska Town	8.85
The Refuge	9.03	Prestwick	8.84
River Oaks	8.95	Bunker Hills	8.76
Mississippi Dunes	8.89	The Links at Northfork	8.73
Majestic Oaks (Signature)	8.87	Wild Marsh	8.73

Hacker's Favorite Winners

TOP TEN

USABILITY (out of 10 points)

Applewood Hills	9.32	River Oaks	9.01
Elk River	9.23	Wild Marsh	9.01
Chaska Town	9.19	Emerald Greens (silv/plat)	8.94
The Refuge	9.13	The Links at Northfork	8.90
Cedar Creek	9.03	Stonebrooke	8.87

NOTE: *Applewood Hills, Hayden Hills and Gem Lake Hills are actually executive eighteens. Who said a course had to be par 72 to be good?*

FACILITY (out of 10 points)

The Refuge	9.16	Chaska Town	8.73
Mississippi Dunes	9.15	Legends	8.69
Crystal Lake	9.01	Stonebrooke	8.68
Braemar	8.99	Rush Creek	8.56
Deer Run	8.98	The Links at Northfork	8.36

NOTE: *Courses that did not have a driving range were marked down in value scores. Where do you warm up that driver?*

VALUE (out of 10 points)

Hiawatha	7.89	Hollydale	7.59
Hayden Hills	7.85	The Ponds	7.47
Elk River	7.64	Rum River Hills	7.46
Cedar Creek	7.64	Baker National	7.42
Tanners Brook	7.62	Southern Hills	7.39

Courses by Name

Course	City	Region	Page
Afton Alps	Afton	SE	90
Applewood Hills	Stillwater	NE	48
Baker National	Medina	SW	62
Bellwood Oaks	Hastings	SE	91
Bluff Creek	Chanhassen	SW	63
Boulder Pointe	Elko	SW	64
Braemar	Edina	SW	65
Brookview	Golden Valley	SW	66
Bunker Hills	Coon Rapids	NW	22
Cedar Creek	Albertville	NW	23
Chaska Town	Chaska	SW	67
Chomonix	Lino Lakes	NE	49
Columbia	Minneapolis	SW	68
Como	St. Paul	SE	92
Country Air	Lake Elmo	SE	93
Crystal Lake	Lakeville	SW	69
Dahlgreen	Chaska	SW	70
Daytona	Dayton	NW	24
Deer Run	Victoria	SW	71
Dwan	Bloomington	SW	72
Eagle Valley	Woodbury	SE	94
Edinburgh USA	Brooklyn Park	NW	25
Elk River	Elk River	NW	26
Elm Creek	Plymouth	NW	27
Emerald Greens (brnz/gold)	Hastings	SE	95
Emerald Greens (silv/plat)	Hastings	SE	96
Fountain Valley	Farmington	SE	97
Fox Hollow	St. Michael	SW	73
Francis A. Gross	Minneapolis	SW	74
Gem Lake Hills	White Bear Lake	NE	50

Courses by Name

Course	City	Region	Page
Goodrich	Maplewood	SE	98
Greenhaven	Anoka	NW	28
Hayden Hills	Dayton	NW	29
Heritage Links	Lakeville	SW	75
Hiawatha	Minneapolis	SW	76
Hidden Greens	Hastings	SE	99
Hidden Haven	Cedar	NE	51
Highland National	St. Paul	SE	100
Hollydale	Plymouth	NW	30
Hyland Greens	Bloomington	SW	77
Inver Wood	Inv Grove Hghts	SE	101
Keller	St. Paul	SE	102
Lakeview	Mound	SW	78
Legends	Prior Lake	SW	79
Les Bolstad	St. Paul	SE	103
Logger's Trail	Stillwater	NE	52
Majestic Oaks (Crossroads)	Ham Lake	NW	31
Majestic Oaks (Signature)	Ham Lake	NW	32
Manitou Ridge	White Bear Lake	NE	53
Meadowbrook	Hopkins	SW	80
Mississippi Dunes	Cottage Grove	SE	104
Monticello	Monticello	NW	33
Oak Glen	Stillwater	NE	54
Oak Marsh	Oakdale	SE	105
Oneka Ridge	White Bear Lake	NE	55
Parkview	Eagan	SE	106
Pebble Creek	Becker	NW	34
Phalen Park	St. Paul	SE	107
Pheasant Acres	Rogers	NW	35
Pioneer Creek	Maple Plain	SW	81

Courses by Name

Courses by City

Courses by City

City	Course	Region	Page
Forest Lake	Tanners Brook	NE	59
Golden Valley	Brookview	SW	66
Ham Lake	Majestic Oaks (Crossroads)	NW	31
Ham Lake	Majestic Oaks (Signature)	NW	32
Hastings	Bellwood Oaks	SE	91
Hastings	Emerald Greens (brnz/gold)	SE	95
Hastings	Emerald Greens (silv/plat)	SE	96
Hastings	Hidden Greens	SE	99
Hopkins	Meadowbrook	SW	80
Invr Grove Hghts	Inver Wood	SE	101
Jordan	Ridges at Sand Creek	SW	82
Lake Elmo	Country Air	SE	93
Lakeville	Crystal Lake	SW	69
Lakeville	Heritage Links	SW	75
Lino Lakes	Chomonix	NE	49
Maple Grove	Rush Creek	NE	56
Maple Plain	Pioneer Creek	SW	81
Maplewood	Goodrich	SE	98
Medina	Baker National	SW	62
Minneapolis	Columbia	SW	68
Minneapolis	Francis A. Gross	SW	74
Minneapolis	Hiawatha	SW	76
Minneapolis	Theodore Wirth	SW	86
Monticello	Monticello	NW	33
Mound	Lakeview	SW	78
Oak Grove	The Refuge	NW	42
Oakdale	Oak Marsh	SE	105
Otsego	Riverwood National	NW	36
Otsego	Vintage	NW	44

Courses by City

Twin Cities Courses

Bunker Hills	Pebble Creek
Cedar Creek	Pheasant Acres
Daytona	Riverwood National
Edinburgh USA	Rum River Hills
Elk River	Shamrock
Elm Creek	Sundance
Greenhaven	The Links at Northfork
Hayden Hills	The Ponds
Hollydale	The Refuge
Majestic Oaks (Crossroads)	Viking Meadows
Majestic Oaks (Signature)	Vintage
Monticello	Wild Marsh

Minnesota is the only State to have hosted every one of the 17 championships conducted by the U.S. Golf Association.

BUNKER HILLS

12800 Bunker Prairie Road
Coon Rapids, MN 55448
Clubhouse: 763-755-4141
Golf Shop: 763-755-4141
Type: Public   Par: 36/36/36

www.bunkerhillsgolf.com

Tees	Men's	Women's	Yards
North/East - White	69.7/130	75.6/137	6159
North/East - Blue	71.5/133	77.8/142	6558
East/West - White	70.6/128	76.7/137	6321
East/West - Blue	72.1/130	78.5/140	6648
West/North - White	70.5/133	76.5/140	6278
West/North - Blue	72.4/137	78.8/145	6700

Region: Twin Cities

Course Rating

HOSPITALITY	8.90
PLAYABILITY	8.76
USABILITY	8.52
FACILITY	8.19
VALUE	6.83

P

OVERALL SCORE
847

Greens Fee: $38.00 (weekend)
1/2 Cart Fee: $14.00 (weekend)

Looking for an exceptional course? Then head to Bunker Hills Golf Course in Coon Rapids, Minnesota, located just west of Highway 65 on Highway 242. The course sports 27 holes of golf, simply named West, North and East. The course has been host to a wide array of tournaments from the Senior PGA Tour to Minnesota High School state boys and girls tournaments.

Once you start playing you can see that although they have a lot of trees, they are trimmed fairly high and the grass in the open area is mowed to a very playable length. When you get to the greens you'll find that they are large, sloped and very fast. The greens will test you, especially if you find yourself on the high side. As in the name of the course, you'll also find they put in lots of bunkers. If you land in one, they are filled with some of the nicest sand that you can play out of. One thing you will find is that they can be reached on a lot of the holes with a driver, so be aware of your options. Throughout the course you will find that the tee boxes are well set up, with benches for a quick rest, trash bins and ball washers. They also have good locations for the restroom facilities.

This would be a great course for anyone to walk, with holes close by each other and with the gentle roll of the fairways. The pro shop has everything you will need, at the price you would expect at such a course. They have a nice driving range, as well as a good putting green located right next to the first tee box, so if you want to do some practicing before your round, you won't have far to go when the starter calls you.

There are GPS on the carts for distances, but if you are walking you'll have to look for sprinkler heads for your information. The clubhouse has a bar and grill as well as a restaurant. It also has a lot of history on its walls inside so take time to look around after your round. Bunker Hills is a great facility, the service and people are friendly and helpful, and you will see they take pride in their course the moment you get there.

CEDAR CREEK

5700 Jason Avenue
Albertville, MN 55301
Clubhouse: 763-497-8245
Golf Shop: 763-497-8245
Type: Public   Par: 71

www.cedarcreekmn.com

Tees	Men's	Women's	Yards
Red	62.9/115	66.9/114	4725
White	67.3/123	72.4/125	5715
Blue	68.8/127	74.3/129	6060

Course Rating

HOSPITALITY	8.43
PLAYABILITY	8.41
USABILITY	9.03
FACILITY	7.02
VALUE	7.64

U
V

OVERALL SCORE
825

Greens Fee: $36.00 (weekend)
1/2 Cart Fee: $14.00 (weekend)

Attention hackers, play it now and score well, wait five years and your score will certainly go up! This environmentally friendly golf course is located in Albertville, Minnesota, just two miles from Interstate 94 and just south of the Albertville Outlet Mall.

Opened in 1999, this 18-hole course with driving range and two practice greens is still in its youth. The course's length is short, playing only 5715 yards from the white tees and 6060 from the blues, although the course's layout has a professional design feel to it. Using natural wetlands to line some of the fairways and also forcing you on some holes to tee off over the wetlands, it makes for a stiff challlenge. The lush fairways are tree-lined, but the trees are small, and the rough is very forgiving. To test your accuracy, it seems every hole has strategically placed sand traps that will catch your errant drives or snag your approach shots to the nicely sized greens.

The pro shop with two pros on staff and a wide range of accessories is very well equipped. There is food and bar service in the clubhouse. It has a great lunch menu and a large patio overlooking the 18th green. The course has five different leagues: men's, women's, senior and junior leagues, as well as a couple's league on Friday.

Put this course near the top of your must-play list and with five more years of maturity, Cedar Creek Golf Course will challenge even the top golfers.

Tim Herron's grandfather, Carson Lee Herron, played in the U.S. Open in 1934 and his father, also named Carson, played in the U.S. Open in 1963.

DAYTONA

14730 Lawndale Lane
Dayton, MN 55327
Clubhouse: 763-427-6110
Golf Shop: 763-427-6110
Type: Public   Par: 72

www.daytonagolfclub.com

Tees	Men's	Women's	Yards
Red		71.0/121	5365
Gold	66.9/116	72.4/124	5614
White	70.4/124	76.9/135	6377

Region: Twin Cities

Course Rating

HOSPITALITY   7.76
PLAYABILITY   5.64
USABILITY   6.40
FACILITY   5.04
VALUE   4.59

OVERALL SCORE
613

Greens Fee: $34.00 (weekend)
1/2 Cart Fee: $14.50 (weekend)

Surrounded by corn fields, Daytona Golf Club, located in Dayton, Minnesota, is a country club, with the emphasis on country. A bit off the beaten path, it also has an indoor tennis facility with a metal roof that appears to be used more extensively in the cooler months.

The two-story clubhouse is nicely appointed with a pro shop, full oak bar, a number of flat screen TVs and a grill with a nice selection of entrees. Its layout flows nicely onto the course and the first tee is only steps from the pro shop where you check in and golf carts are just outside the door. One thing missing was a driving range, even though something called a driving range appears to be located on land adjacent to the facility.

Listed at 6377 yards from the tips, all the holes do not boast tees at that length so it really plays about 6100 yards. Some courses play longer than their length, but this course really feels shorter attesting to the listed rating of par 72, but the USGA only scoring it at par 70.4. Also, because it has very few hazards and trees, most holes are wide open with large areas to land an errant tee shot, making this a very easy course to play. Although the yardage markers were good, the course signage as well as the cart paths were very poor. Other weaknesses are that the course has no water coolers and we counted only two portable bathrooms.

The golf course conditions show that it needs some attention and maintenance. Everywhere could be found evidence that the course is rarely if ever watered. With the exception of the greens, which were in very nice shape, the rest of the course from the tee boxes to the fairways was dry and the ground was hard, making a ball roll a good distance before stopping. The layout also could use some improvement by adding water, rough and more sand bunkers. Right now it is relatively unimaginative with only a couple of doglegs breaking up the monotony.

This facility's strongest suit is the clubhouse. If you are looking for a nice, mid-priced meal after your round, it's a nice place to linger. As to the course, it needs a facelift and is not a great value for the money.

EDINBURGH USA

8700 Edinbrook Crossing
Brooklyn Park, MN 55443
Clubhouse: 763-315-8500
Golf Shop: 763-315-8550
Type: Public   Par: 72
www.edinburghusa.org

Course Rating

HOSPITALITY	7.78
PLAYABILITY	7.68
USABILITY	6.43
FACILITY	7.60
VALUE	5.15

NORTHWEST

OVERALL SCORE
719

Greens Fee: $50.00 (weekend)
1/2 Cart Fee: $17.00 (weekend)

Tees	Men's	Women's	Yards
Red		71.6/133	5255
White	69.7/135	74.5/139	5858
Blue	72.1/139		6383
Black	74.2/149		6867

Approaching the clubhouse at Edinburgh USA, you may feel like you are entering a plush country club atmosphere in the heart of Brooklyn Park. Luckily, Edinburgh USA is reasonably priced and was constructed with public funds. It is also consistently rated as one of the top 100 public courses in the USA. The huge, stone clubhouse contains conference rooms, banquet rooms, a pro shop, locker rooms, bar and restaurant. The bar features good happy-hour specials and great appetizers as well as a full menu. You can order lunch from a phone system located at the 9th hole and have it ready for you when you arrive at the clubhouse.

This is one of the most challenging courses one can expect to play. Accuracy is key and strategy a must. There are five lakes on the course and somewhere between 70–80 traps. Trees protect the edges of the fairways on many holes. Bring plenty of balls when you come to play and consider yourself fortunate indeed if you don't need them.

As the course is considered a championship course, there are four sets of tee boxes on each hole. The fairways, greens and traps are in excellent shape and the cart paths and signage are adequate for finding your way from one hole to the next.

The course is within the hacker's budget and the food and beverages are reasonably priced. There are clocks set up around the course to time your progress and encourage those that may be slow to speed up their games. The ranger is quite regular in his rounds to ensure proper course conduct and play speed. If you are a walker, the course should still play about the same time as it is gently rolling and not too exhausting to walk.

We found the staff to be very friendly and cooperative and other golfers well mannered. The only problem encountered was with the workers on the fairways and tee boxes continuing to work while we were teeing off. Seeing as they were laying sod in the middle of the fairway, we can only assume that they felt unthreatened by our tremendous drives.

ELK RIVER

20015 Elk Lake Road
Elk River, MN 55330
Clubhouse: 763-441-4111
Golf Shop: 763-441-4111
Type: Semi-Private   Par: 72

www.elkrivercc.com

Tees	Men's	Women's	Yards
Red		72.7/123	5590
White	70.1/123	75.7/130	6140
Blue	71.6/126		6480

Region: Twin Cities

Course Rating

HOSPITALITY	8.44
PLAYABILITY	9.20
USABILITY	9.23
FACILITY	7.88
VALUE	7.64

**P
U
V**

OVERALL SCORE
866

Greens Fee: $33.00 (weekend)
1/2 Cart Fee: $13.15 (weekend)

Blind tee shots, doglegs and small, fast greens! If you want to challenge your short game, Elk River Country Club in Elk River, Minnesota, is the course to give it to you. Located a half-hour drive north of the Twin Cities just off of Highway 10, Elk River Country Club has it all, from a professionally run pro shop along with a teaching pro to help you on their driving range.

The course staff were very friendly as were the other golfers. We decided to play from the back tees, as looking at the scorecard 6480 yards seemed somewhat short from these tees. The course does play short, as with a good drive, 220–260 yards, you have a short iron shot to all of the par-4 greens. The obstacle was making a good drive! We seemed to be faced with a lot of blind tee shots and doglegs while standing at the tee box. Hint #1—don't play for money if playing someone with course knowledge!

The course, tees, fairways and greens were in great shape. You can easily see your ball in the rough, and the trees are trimmed up allowing for an easy recovery shot. Being that the holes played short there had to be a catch and it is the small, fast greens. The greens do not have many slopes to them but they are small and they are fast! Hint # 2—practice the bump and run and your short chip shots.

For the golfer that enjoys the game when they walk, this course is very favorable. There are only a couple holes with a major change in elevation from tee to green; and the next hole's tees are not that far from the previous green. Also we never experienced everyone else's errant shots from other fairways due to the large trees that line each hole.

On-course facilities were a bit slim, as it wasn't until after the 7th hole that a porta-potty and drink machine were located. Finishing our round in a fast four hours, we easily found a table on the shaded patio of the clubhouse. The restaurant staff was very pleasant and the food was quick, plentiful and very tasty. If you want to challenge your short game or entertain the whole family, Elk River Country Club will fulfill all of your needs.

ELM CREEK

19000 Highway 55
Plymouth, MN 55446
Clubhouse: 763-478-6716
Golf Shop: 763-478-6716
Type: Public   Par: 70
www.elmcreekgc.com

Course Rating

HOSPITALITY	8.02
PLAYABILITY	7.30
USABILITY	7.87
FACILITY	7.31
VALUE	6.02

OVERALL SCORE
747

Tees	Men's	Women's	Yards
Red		68.0/117	4728
Yellow	66.0/120	70.9/123	5245
White	67.5/123	72.7/127	5577
Blue	69.0/125		5891

Greens Fee: $32.00 (weekend)
1/2 Cart Fee: $14.00 (weekend)

NORTHWEST

If you played Elm Creek Golf Course five years ago, you might have remembered it as one of those courses that was the first to open and the last to close in an attempt to squeeze every dollar from the golf season. Well, things have changed. According to the course's general manager, since new owners took over in 2004, they have continued to improve both the on- and off-course experience with a methodical investment leading to better manicured fairways and greens. You also won't find them open late into November any longer so they are able to preserve the course for the following year.

Traveling on Highway 55, Elm Creek Golf Course, just on the western edge of Plymouth, Minnesota, is only accessible from the east. The layout of the facility is very compact and you can hit the front door and find your cart in just a few steps. The course, because it has nowhere to expand, unfortunately doesn't have a driving range, but does have a nice putting green.

Elm Creek, from which the course gets its name, makes its presence known at a handful of holes where the creek snakes alongside or through the fairway. Although the course is relatively short at 5891 yards, it makes up for it with wickedly difficult fairways and challenging approach shots that might tempt you to try and drive the green. This is not a "grip it and rip it" course; it is all about course management and shot selection.

Like all courses, Elm Creek has its own quirks. Since some of the holes cross each other, the signage can be a bit confusing so make sure you check out the map before venturing out. Also, yardage markers are a bit hard to see in spots and because of significant elevation changes on some holes, it will be important to know when you have a blind approach shot.

With close proximity to the Twin Cities as well as excellent pricing, the course is very popular with groups and has a nice clubhouse that allows for catering and an open patio for barbecues. It also is priced right with rates from $19 to $32 depending upon the time and day.

NORTHWEST

GREENHAVEN

2800 Greenhaven Road
Anoka, MN 55303
Clubhouse: 763-576-2965
Golf Shop: 763-576-2970
Type: Public   Par: 71
www.greenhavengolfcourse.com

Tees	Men's	Women's	Yards
Red		71.0/123	5333
Yellow		75.0/132	6059
Yellow/Gold	69.5//128		6059
Blue	70.5/130		6276

Region: Twin Cities

Course Rating

HOSPITALITY   8.63
PLAYABILITY   7.59
USABILITY   7.63
FACILITY   6.65
VALUE   6.91

OVERALL SCORE
765

Greens Fee: $31.00 (weekend)
1/2 Cart Fee: $14.00 (weekend)

Folks traveling along Highway 10 on their way to the lake may miss Greenhaven Golf Course in Anoka. Pigeonholed between a frontage road and railroad tracks in the heart of a developed city, the course is landlocked. Only 6300 yards from the tips, the course does all it can to maximize the playing experience and has used the land to such a degree that you'll find very little rough in which to lose your ball.

Arriving at the course makes you feel you are playing at a country club. The large clubhouse has a full bar, grill, and outdoor seating as well as space to host weddings. Even breakfast is available if you've just finished an early round. One surprise was the brand new golf carts.

Although the course is short, it does its best to try to challenge the typical golfer. Even with these additions, the course still feels tired and limited. Big weaknesses are the cart paths and signage. The cart paths are sporadic and where the asphalt ends and the dirt starts, watch for potholes. On-course signage is quite weak and unless you follow the white lines painted on the course, you might lose your way to the next hole. Another weakness is the practice area where you hit "floater" balls that land in a pond. When we were there the practice range had run out of balls so we were only able to practice our putting.

The course is very walkable and has benches at each hole, but shade is a rare commodity so take sunblock. Also, because of its location within the city of Anoka, the Highway 10 frontage road and a very busy and loud train track line define the edge of the course on two sides. The frontage road is so close that on #17 you can hear drive-through orders being placed at a nearby Taco Bell and if you want, get your own Mexican food fix before you tee off.

If you are looking for an inexpensive round of golf on a course that accommodates short hitters, Greenhaven is your course. If you want a better layout that provides more challenge in a more quiet location, another course might be a better option.

HAYDEN HILLS Exec. 18

13150 Deerwood Lane North
Dayton, MN 55327
Clubhouse: 763-421-0060
Golf Shop: 763-421-0060
Type: Public   Par: 62
no website available

Tees	Men's	Women's	Yards
White	56.7/80	56.2/78	3054
Blue	57.6/82	57.9/82	3368

Course Rating

HOSPITALITY	8.23
PLAYABILITY	6.32
USABILITY	5.73
FACILITY	6.12
VALUE	7.85

V

OVERALL SCORE
680

Greens Fee: $22.50 (weekend)
1/2 Cart Fee: included in fee

NORTHWEST

Need to practice on your short game? If so, Hayden Hills Executive Golf Course in Dayton, Minnesota, is a great course to do so. With one par 5, six par 4s, and twelve par 3s, the course plays to a total of 3368 yards. This is a great walking course (very flat) that features a nice mixture of trees, water and sand to make it a bit of a challenge but also very forgiving. The rough is short and it is difficult to lose balls on this course. The play offers some interesting challenges on doglegs (should I go over the trees for a shot at the green or go down the center of the fairway for an easy approach?) and a couple of holes where a golfer can hit over water or play it safe. The course has a nice screen of trees and shrubbery that enhances the play with very little visibility of the bordering housing subdivisions. Gives you a feeling of a nice walk in the country.

The course is fairly easy to find. It is located off of County Road 121. There is also easy access off of County Road 81 (Maple Grove) or Highway 169 (Champlin). Keep an eye open for Deerwood Lane as the signage isn't the best and the entrance isn't seen from the road until you get to the end of Deerwood Lane.

The course has a putting and pitching green just outside the dated but clean clubhouse. There is no golf pro and no pro shop for clothing items. The clubhouse features clean restrooms, snack bar and a large community room for seating.   Staff are friendly, players courteous, and the snack bar offers standard fare at reasonable prices. Eighteen holes and cart for $22 is very reasonable.

This is a good course to start the season and get your irons ready for the regulation courses to follow.

Town & Country Club, a private golf club in St. Paul, opened in 1893, is the nation's second oldest golf course and has been in continuous operation to this day.

HOLLYDALE

4710 Holly Lane North
Plymouth, MN 55446
Clubhouse: 763-559-9847
Golf Shop: 763-559-9847
Type: Public   Par: 71
www.hollydalegolf.com

Region: Twin Cities

Course Rating

HOSPITALITY	8.33
PLAYABILITY	6.94
USABILITY	7.46
FACILITY	6.44
VALUE	7.59

V

Tees	Men's	Women's	Yards
Red		69.3/116	5128
Mixed		72.5/123	5666
White	68.8/116	74.0/126	5980
Blue	69.6/118		6160

OVERALL SCORE
738

Greens Fee: $29.00 (weekend)
1/2 Cart Fee: $13.00 (weekend)

Hollydale Golf Course in Plymouth, Minnesota, is what would be called a ground-strokes course—a good place to work on your basic shots with little chance of running into any trouble. The 6160-yard course is compact. So compact there is very little need for directional signage. The fairways are wide open with the only hazards being mature trees. There are few if any bunkers and only a couple of holes require hitting near or over water.

Three tee boxes exist on most holes and the course has little if any cart paths. Hole distances are easy to find and the next tee box is only a short distance from the previous green. The greens, although reasonably large, don't require a difficult read because most are very flat with little contour. They were also, at the time of this review, oddly slow and probably in need of aeration.

This is an extremely walkable course because of its lack of length, compact facility and very few elevation changes. The driving range, which sits in the middle of the course, is reasonably priced and the putting area and parking lot are very close to the clubhouse. If you are looking for a fancy place to stop after your round, the clubhouse isn't the place. It is very utilitarian with a small kitchen, sitting area and check-in. The food offerings are very basic and what you expect for golf course cuisine. Check-in is manual and there are no online tee times available from their website.

Unlike area courses that might have a bigger name or are more popular, Hollydale is a little oasis situated in residential Plymouth. Think of a miniature New York's Central Park. It isn't expensive to play here, generally isn't busy and it is close by for those living on the west side of the Twin Cities.

This won't become your favorite course that you play every weekend, but the course is extremely hacker friendly and something you'd want to play on occasion when you want to work on your game. Hollydale prices itself as a good value while still keeping it just enough of a challenge to let the golfer feel good when he/she has finished for the day.

MAJESTIC OAKS
(Crossroads Course)

701 Bunker Lake Boulevard
Ham Lake, MN 55304
Clubhouse: 763-755-2140
Golf Shop: 763-755-2142
Type: Public   Par: 72
www.majesticoaksgolfclub.com

Course Rating

HOSPITALITY	8.15
PLAYABILITY	7.33
USABILITY	6.57
FACILITY	6.90
VALUE	6.54

NORTHWEST

OVERALL SCORE
724

Tees	Men's	Women's	Yards
Silver		68.9/122	4849
Black	69.4/126		5879
Gold	71.8/131		6396

Greens Fee: $32.00 (weekend)
1/2 Cart Fee: $15.00 (weekend)

Majestic Oaks, located just off of Highway 65 in Ham Lake, offers two 18-hole courses, Crossroads and Signature, and an additional executive 9-hole course. The pro shop is a short walk from the parking lot. A large putting green is situated just outside the clubhouse, and another putting green adjoins the driving range where you can hit a bucket of balls for $7. You'll need to head to the clubhouse to use the restroom, since the pro shop doesn't have any facilities. At the club-house you'll find a relaxing atmosphere with areas for sitting, a bar, spacious restaurant with an extensive menu and cheerful, friendly staff.

The Crossroads course is fairly level and the distances between holes is such that one can easily walk 18 holes without a problem. Reservations may be made four days in advance, but can't be made through the course's website.

Signs leading to the first Crossroads tee and driving range are lacking, so your best bet is to follow the cart paths in the general direction of the course. The tee boxes' conditions indicate much use; the fairways are in good shape; and the greens look fantastic. On a few holes, golfers may want to lay up in front of a haz-ard to insure an easier second shot. Houses surround nearly the entire course, but golfers are permitted to retrieve errant shots from the lawns. For the most part, the houses do not come into play for the average golfer.

Consider this fair warning—there are no porta-potties on Crossroads until the end of the 9th hole, and golfers don't come near the clubhouse until the 18th hole has been completed. Golfers may want to carry their own beverages since the bever-age cart service was scarce when this writer was there. Majestic Oaks hosts many tournaments and events, so staff may have been busy elsewhere on the courses on this particular day.

All in all, Majestic Oaks Crossroads provides a walkable, challenging golf experi-ence that the average duffer would find enjoyable. The clubhouse offers a com-fortable spot to discuss one's great shots over appetizers or a meal and a wide choice of beverages.

MAJESTIC OAKS
(Signature Course)

701 Bunker Lake Boulevard
Ham Lake, MN 55304
Clubhouse: 763-755-2140
Golf Shop: 763-755-2142
Type: Public   Par: 72
www.majesticoaksgolfclub.com

Region: Twin Cities

Course Rating

HOSPITALITY	9.05
PLAYABILITY	8.87
USABILITY	7.76
FACILITY	8.13
VALUE	6.24

H
P

OVERALL SCORE
832

Greens Fee: $36.00 (weekend)
1/2 Cart Fee: $15.00 (weekend)

Tees	Men's	Women's	Yards
Silver		71.6/124	5268
Black	70.8/127	76.0/133	6060
Gold	72.5/131		6442
Green	74.1/134		6792
Blue	75.5/137		7107

Majestic Oaks is quite easy to get to. It is located about one mile west of Highway 65 on Bunker Lake Boulevard in Ham Lake. It is home to an executive course and two 18-hole courses. It also consists of a large complex able to host corporate outings, weddings, and banquets. The food service available was in the bar and grill. There was a good variety of food at a reasonable cost and good service.

We found it strange that the pro shop was detached from the main complex and was small and minimally stocked. The staff was polite but exhibited a somber mood. Another oddity was the golf carts were without tops/roofs and no GPS. When it is hot and humid it would be rather uncomfortable riding in the open carts. The putting green is in close proximity to the pro shop, carts and the first and tenth tees of the course. The driving range is also close by and was well maintained.

We were impressed by the whole experience. Hole routing was excellent with cart paths that easily routed you around the course. The cart paths were somewhat weathered, but acceptable. Signage at the tees and getting you from greens to the next tee was very good. The greens were large and fair with few ball marks, but a little on the slow side. They probably need to be aerated. The fairways were in very good shape and generous widths, and the rough consistent at a minimal height. A beverage cart came by three times during our round.

The website is mostly geared to event bookings and food service. They do have an area to book tee times online, but it was very cumbersome the few times we tried to use it so we ended up calling for a tee time. The greens fee structure is an excellent value for the quality of the course and the overall experience.

The Signature course has been around a long time and we believe it is a hidden gem in the Twin Cities.

MONTICELLO

1209 Golf Course Road, PO Box 651
Monticello, MN 55362
Clubhouse: 763-295-4653
Golf Shop: 763-295-4653
Type: Semi-Private   Par: 71
www.montigolf.com

Course Rating

HOSPITALITY	8.28
PLAYABILITY	7.80
USABILITY	7.30
FACILITY	6.65
VALUE	6.60

OVERALL SCORE
753

Greens Fee: $39.00 (weekend)
1/2 Cart Fee: $15.00 (weekend)

NORTHWEST

Tees	Men's	Women's	Yards
Red		70.3/119	5085
Green		71.9/123	5385
Yellow	68.6/120	74.2/128	5793
White	70.3/123		6157
Blue	71.6/126		6453

We were definitely skeptical of the Monticello Country Club's website promise that our round of golf would be "worth the drive," but the hour-long gas guzzler northwest to this semi-private course definitely proved worthwhile. Monticello is a reasonably priced course for players at all levels.

With mature trees and a nice combination of obstacles, including ponds, well-maintained sand traps, even a bubbling brook that tangles through two holes, Monticello does present its challenges. However, you do not have to be a thinker or a precision specialist here.

The greens were large and ready for the occasional three putt. Many had multiple levels and all played extremely fast. This may have been partly attributable to the colder, dryer weather at the time. The course has a very nice practice area including a large putting green, a coin-operated driving range close to the first tee box and a practice area complete with sand bunker. This provided a great opportunity to warm up before the round.

Inside, the clubhouse is quite nice with plenty of space to sit, a gas fireplace and a full concession area. We almost needed a hammer to flush the urinal in the men's room but that was a minor issue in the overall clubhouse impression. Staff said good morning and were friendly.

There were a few negatives to our round. At least four holes on the front nine were accompanied by the sounds of Interstate 94. You might not care and it might not affect your game, but the cars and trucks will be whizzing by. We also found that the tee boxes were solid, as if the grounds crew had prepped to lay a brick patio and instead chose to put grass down.

Overall, if you're looking to have fun and hack away at a nice course, on a nice pace without the expense found at other courses, you might find the drive to Monticello to be worth it.

PEBBLE CREEK

Region: Twin Cities

14000 Clubhouse Lane
Becker, MN 55308
Clubhouse: 763-263-4653
Golf Shop: 763-263-4653
Type: Public   Par: 36/36/36
www.pebblecreekgolf.com

Course Rating

HOSPITALITY	7.50
PLAYABILITY	7.99
USABILITY	7.27
FACILITY	6.87
VALUE	6.35

Tees	Men's	Women's	Yards
Red/White (middle)	68.3/119	73.7/126	5756
Red/White (champ)	73.3/140		6872
White/Blue (middle)	67.9/119	73.1/128	5639
White/Blue (champ)	72.6/136		6696
Blue/Red (middle)	68.7/122	73.7/129	5803
Blue/Red (champ)	73.0/139		6818

OVERALL SCORE
739

Greens Fee: $42.00 (weekend)
1/2 Cart Fee: $14.00 (weekend)

If you are planning a trip to St. Cloud, Pebble Creek in Becker, Minnesota, might be a stop you'd want to make on your way. One of the highlights is the creek that flows throughout many of the holes, hence the name. Pebble Creek is large enough that some might call it a river, and it twists and turns to flow alongside and across many of the holes in a way that is quite beautiful. The course is also bordered by an old-growth forest of leafy trees, which is also very stunning and adds a sense of calming peace.

What does not help with that calming peace is the huge lack of signage. We were constantly guessing which way to go for the next hole, and were wrong many times. Distance to the pin was always a toss-up, and finding the correct tee box just seemed to be harder than it needed to be. Luckily, the pace of play was pretty ideal, as there was wide spacing between tee times on a rather nice Sunday afternoon.

One feature of this course is the choice to play two of three 9-hole courses. Each is really challenging, with constant hazards and somewhat narrow fairways, so hackers had better bring their A-game or be ready for some high scores.

The banquet facility and full-service bar upstairs in the clubhouse are really nice, with a few flat screen TVs and a deck for relaxing after your round. This reviewer was the only customer in the place and the girl behind the counter seemed a bit disinterested in providing service. The food selection was a little scarce as well. Admittedly, however, an establishment cannot be judged based on the service from one employee alone. In contrast, the on-course cart girl was Johnny-on-the-spot, with a very friendly disposition.

All in all, this really is a beautiful course, and will certainly flush out the most accurate golfer in your group. The biggest hang-up might be the value component. The greens and fairway conditions are average, so at $56 to ride 18 holes on the weekend, there are certainly options out there that may give a bigger bang for the buck.

PHEASANT ACRES

10705 County Road 116
Rogers, MN 55374
Clubhouse: 763-428-8244
Golf Shop: 763-428-8244
Type: Public   Par: 72
www.pheasantacresgolf.com

Tees	Men's	Women's	Yards
Red		69.1/118	5082
Gold	67.3/115		5632
White	69.3/119		6099
Blue	71.2/122		6523

Region: Twin Cities

Course Rating

HOSPITALITY	8.54
PLAYABILITY	8.33
USABILITY	7.88
FACILITY	7.94
VALUE	7.16

OVERALL SCORE
812

NORTHWEST

Greens Fee: $34.00 (weekend)
1/2 Cart Fee: $14.00 (weekend)

Located in the northwest corner of Hennepin County, Pheasant Acres Golf Course in Rogers, Minnesota, is easy to locate and fun to play. Easiest access is from Highway 55, north on County Road 116 until you see the course on your left. You can also access the course by driving Highway 94 to County Road 30 (Maple Grove) west to County Road 116 and north to the course.

Driving range, chipping green and putting green are located adjacent to the clubhouse and the clubhouse itself offers a full-service restaurant and bar. While relatively small, the clubhouse makes use of all of its space. A pro shop is on-site with the typical selection of clothing and gear. PGA Professional Instructor Steve Fessler is available for private and group lessons. There are a number of various leagues one can join and always a special for greens fees.

The 18-hole course has some 30 traps and 16 ponds as well as some wooded areas. Roughs are well groomed and a ball in the rough is easily located. The course is fairly easy to walk with only a couple of uphill stretches and those are gradual in slope. A nice mixture of well-placed challenges are offered to the golfer, but strategic play should keep one out of trouble through most of the course. The course offers outhouses and toilets at well-spaced points. There are coin-operated pop machines at midpoints on each nine. The beverage cart is usually circling the course as well.

When we golfed this course we found the staff always friendly and the other golfers cordial. This course offers a decent challenge to sharpen your skills at rates that are as competitive as any in the Metro area. If you are anywhere near Rogers, stop in at Pheasant Acres Golf Course.

Bois de Sioux Golf Course is the only public golf course in the nation to have holes in two different states: nine in Breckenridge, Minnesota, and nine in Wahpeton, North Dakota.

RIVERWOOD NATIONAL

Region: Twin Cities

10444 95th Street NE
Otsego, MN 55362
Clubhouse: 763-271-5000
Golf Shop: 763-271-5000
Type: Public   Par: 72
www.riverwoodnational.com

Course Rating

HOSPITALITY	7.62
PLAYABILITY	7.25
USABILITY	6.32
FACILITY	6.05
VALUE	6.08

Tees	Men's	Women's	Yards
Red		67.8/115	4722
White	69.4/131	75.3/131	6064
Blue	70.8/135		6376
Black	73.7/140		7012

OVERALL SCORE
682

Greens Fee: $35.00 (weekend)
1/2 Cart Fee: $13.00 (weekend)

Just shy of an hour northwest of the cities on Interstate 94 brings you to the growing extended suburban community of Otsego, Minnesota, and the Riverwood National Golf Course. Before you even step on the course, Riverwood does a great job of making you feel like your drive was worthwhile. A great clubhouse, nice facilities and awesome golf carts provide a buffer for any frustration that might get built up while hacking away on the course. Digital scorecard, GPS system and menu hooked into the clubhouse restaurant are just some of the features found within the dashboard of your golf cart, which can be rented for 18 holes on a weekend for a very reasonable $13.

A championship course by title, Riverwood seems to do its best to offer a fair experience to golfers of all skill levels. Though the challenge is there, the course is not overbearingly difficult for golfers with lesser skill sets. The majority of holes offer a safe out for those not willing to roll the dice on a perfect swing, and the room for error is pretty even across the board. There is, however, trouble that can be found, and a couple holes are potential snowmen waiting to happen. Despite this, the course maintains its level of fairness by tending to surround these tougher holes with less demanding ones. This means that even though a couple scores might jump up and bite you, if you can keep your composure and move on to the next tee box with a clear conscience, you have a chance to make up for it on the following hole.

Overall, Riverwood is an enjoyable course. Stepping onto the first tee box you know that the course is not going to roll over for you, but it is also not difficult to the point where you're going to want to bury your seven-iron in a pond after your third straight triple bogey. A welcoming atmosphere and a fair challenge come to mind, and for a little jaunt up Interstate 94 it's not a bad pick for a golfer of any skill level. Plus, a happy hour pit stop at the sports bar conveniently located between the course and Interstate 94 will help turn the story about that cut-slice-tree-green shot you hit on #11 into a reason to come back again.

RUM RIVER HILLS

16659 St. Francis Boulevard
Ramsey, MN 55303
Clubhouse: 763-753-3339
Golf Shop: 763-753-3339
Type: Public   Par: 71

www.rumriverhills.com

Tees	Men's	Women's	Yards
Red		70.4/123	5024
White	68.8/124	74.2/132	5738
Blue	70.4/127	76.3/136	6091
Black	71.4/129		6308

Course Rating

HOSPITALITY	6.65
PLAYABILITY	6.78
USABILITY	7.14
FACILITY	6.97
VALUE	7.46

OVERALL SCORE
691

Greens Fee: $32.00 (weekend)
1/2 Cart Fee: $15.00 (weekend)

NORTHWEST

For those of us located in the Twin Cities, Rum River Hills Golf Club in Ramsey, Minnesota, seems way out there in the country. It is a bit of a drive tucked away on Highway 47, but what really makes it different is that it is a contrast in two parts: the clubhouse and the course.

The clubhouse has the feel of an Elk's Lodge complete with a tiny stage, wood paneling and pull tabs. The course, on the other hand, is picturesque and challenging with more than half the holes having water hazards to contend with. The clubhouse was built when the course opened in 1983 and appears to not have changed since Day One. Designed by noted golf course architect Joel Goldstrand, Rum River Hills is not a flat blue-collar track, but a tree-lined course with lots of water, bunkers and other ways to lose your golf balls. It is much tougher than meets the eye.

The course itself a tale of two nines with the front nine being much tighter than the back. Course management and shot accuracy should be required for the front, and "grip it and rip it" should be called for on the back. The course is nicely manicured and the greens are pristine. The course length at the white tees is only 5738 yards, so if you are a long hitter, you might want to take a step back to the blues. The ladies are taken into consideration here with their own ball washers, granite signage and garbage cans, touches not often seen at most courses.

In contrast, the off-course amenities seemed a bit lacking. The parking lot needed a paving, the putting green seemed a bit sparse and the driving range was very basic. The golf carts were older and appeared to not have been cleaned since spring. Although we were part of a small group of golfers that played the course late in the year, the service was weak and we got a cold shoulder in the bar from the locals like we were invading their private club.

Rum River Hills Golf Club's course is really a hidden gem that is worth a visit, but the rest of the golfing experience did little to make us want to return again.

SHAMROCK

19625 Larkin Road
Corcoran, MN 55340
Clubhouse: 763-478-9977
Golf Shop: 763-478-9977
Type: Public   Par: 72
www.shamrockgolfcourse.com

Tees	Men's	Women's	Yards
Red		72.7/117	5793
White	69.1/113	74.8/121	6171
Blue	70.3/115		6423

Course Rating

HOSPITALITY	8.28
PLAYABILITY	6.13
USABILITY	8.38
FACILITY	7.11
VALUE	6.03

OVERALL SCORE
726

Greens Fee: $28.00 (weekend)
1/2 Cart Fee: $16.00 (weekend)

Easily accessible from the northwest side of town, Shamrock Golf Course is located just off County Road 116 (Highway 55) and County Road 10 (Interstate 494) in Corcoran, Minnesota. Course terrain is gently rolling with generous fairways and short rough.

This is an excellent course to work on your game and build a little confidence. Sand comes into play on four holes and water on six holes. An easy course for the walkers, it plays at 6171 yards from the whites and it's hard to lose balls on this course. There is only one porta-potty on the course so it can get a little touch-and-go for those with a sensitive bladder.

There isn't much for signage but the asphalt cart paths make getting from one hole to the next easy. The average hacker should feel good about his/her score by the end of the round.

A family of Trumpeter Swans make their home on the pond just outside the clubhouse. The clubhouse is rather spartan with the average grill fare and beer. The clubhouse staff are friendly and helpful. The clubhouse does have a sheltered deck for relaxing after the round. It also offers some good deals on clubs and grips through a local clubmaker. There is no driving range and a rather small putting area. The course offers senior and junior rates, twilight and midday rates. There is no pro at the course and no lessons offered. Overall it offers competitive fees and an excellent opportunity to hone your shots without the fear of getting into trouble on every shot.

Minnesota was ranked by the National Golf Association in 2005 as the nation's number one golf state based on per capita participation. Wisconsin ranked a close second.

SUNDANCE

15420 113th Avenue North
Dayton, MN 55369
Clubhouse: 763-420-4800
Golf Shop: 763-420-4700
Type: Public   Par: 72

www.sundancegolfbowl.com

Tees	Men's	Women's	Yards
Red		71.6/125	5406
White	69.9/129	75.9/134	6192
Blue	70.9/131		6415

Course Rating

HOSPITALITY	8.42
PLAYABILITY	8.38
USABILITY	8.10
FACILITY	7.60
VALUE	6.75

OVERALL SCORE
805

Greens Fee: $33.00 (weekend)
1/2 Cart Fee: $14.00 (weekend)

NORTHWEST

Sundance Golf and Bowl, located in Dayton, Minnesota, is a full-service facility close to the Metro area with rural rates. Located in northern Hennepin County, Sundance is easily accessible from either County Road 81 (Maple Grove) or Highway 169 (Champlin). Follow County Road 121 to 113th Avenue North (Dehn's Country Manor Restaurant is on the corner) and head west to the clubhouse.

This is a full-service facility with driving range, chipping green, putting green and pro shop. In addition, Fritzy's Sports Bar offers a full menu (Thursday is ladies night when female golfers get a free drink ticket) and there is a banquet facility that seats 275 persons. Sundance also offers a 24-lane bowling facility next door. Be sure to check the course website for online specials and rates before you go or book your tee time online.

The on-course amenities are clean and well managed. The practice areas are located adjacent to the clubhouse for easy access for walkers. The course's slope is gentle so walking is comfortable. Carts are clean and well maintained. The large clubhouse offers a congenial sports bar (Fritzy's) that offers a full menu. The clubhouse also offers a banquet facility for tournaments or private functions. The pro shop offers the full range of services from clothing to clubs to grips. The beverage cart makes regular rounds so your thirst should be satiated.

This is a great course for hackers to hone their game. The fairways are generous in width and the hazards are well placed to reward the accurate shot but allow one to play to the opposite side of the fairways or green to avoid hazards if one doesn't trust the shot that needs to be made. We found the fairways, rough and greens to be well maintained.

Hayden Hills Executive Golf Course (also reviewed in this guide) is a couple of miles down the road. It is a short 18-hole course that can be finished in two hours and makes a good practice course to play prior to your round at Sundance. Makes for a great day of golf finished up by happy hour at Fritzy's Sports Bar.

THE LINKS AT NORTHFORK

Region: Twin Cities

9333 Alpine Drive NW
Ramsey, MN 55303
Clubhouse: 763-241-0506
Golf Shop: 763-241-0506
Type: Public   Par: 72
www.golfthelinks.com

P
U
F

Course Rating

HOSPITALITY	9.01
PLAYABILITY	8.73
USABILITY	8.90
FACILITY	8.36
VALUE	7.24

OVERALL SCORE
863

Tees	Men's	Women's	Yards
Forward	67.0/121	71.9/126	5242
Middle	72.0/131	78.0/138	6344
Back	73.4/133	79.8/142	6653
Champion	74.9/139	81.6/146	6989

Greens Fee: $42.00 (weekend)
1/2 Cart Fee: $14.08 (weekend)

Golf provides a unique opportunity to gather with old friends and to meet new ones, especially when playing with a mixed foursome. The experience is heightened when one is fortunate enough to be paired with a clubhouse member who is intimately familiar with the intricacies of the course. As we learned, such a round-mate is invaluable when playing a course as difficult as The Links at Northfork in Ramsey, Minnesota.

The Links at Northfork is a friendly place for a very challenging round of golf. The course is designed as a traditional links course, long and open with contentious hazards throughout. The rough is long and punishing, leaving little room for errant drives. Water is a predominant risk on 10 of the 18 holes. The Links does not have the deep pothole bunkers you will find at St. Andrew's, but sand is a constant threat regardless of your position on the tee box or in the fairway. Even course veterans respect and fear the strategically placed hazards.

Most top-tier golf courses have a signature aspect that makes them memorable. Aside from its uncommon links design, the signature element at The Links at Northfork is its premier practice facilities. The driving range is conveniently located just steps from the clubhouse with some of the most reasonable rates in the Twin Cities. The Links offers two putting greens and a practice sand trap. However, the most notable component of the practice facilities is the 3-hole primer course. Access to this 3-hole loop is complimentary with any round, adding value to the $42 greens fees and allowing the golfer to walk to the first tee box with full confidence. In addition, the on-course amenities make an otherwise challenging round more comfortable, with water stations every four holes, four sets of tee boxes, ball washers at every hole and an omnipresent beverage cart.

The Links at Northfork is a beautiful golf course with an uncommon design. Its amenities and service are second to none. Although the course is quite difficult, it is "hackable" for the average golfer with the temperament to withstand frustrating hazards and a high score. For a taste of challenging links golf in the Twin Cities, The Links at Northfork is the place to go.

THE PONDS

2881 229th Avenue NW
St. Francis, MN 55070
Clubhouse: 763-753-1100
Golf Shop: 763-753-1100
Type: Public   Par: 36/36/36

www.thepondsgolf.com

Region: Twin Cities

Course Rating

HOSPITALITY	8.15
PLAYABILITY	7.39
USABILITY	8.16
FACILITY	7.40
VALUE	7.47

OVERALL SCORE
774

Greens Fee: $32.00 (weekend)
1/2 Cart Fee: $14.00 (weekend)

NORTHWEST

Tees	Men's	Women's	Yards
Red/White (white)	68.5/127	73.6/129	5744
Red/White (blue)	71.9/134	77.8/137	6493
White/Blue (white)	67.1/128	72.2/129	5532
White/Blue (blue)	72.0/137	78.1/142	6599
Blue/Red (white)	67.9/129	73.1/128	5594
Blue/Red (blue)	72.3/138	78.4/139	6550

On the northern edge of the Twin Cities is a course that will have you telling everyone what a great golfer you are. It's called The Ponds Golf Course and is located about 40 minutes north in St. Francis, Minnesota. Its 27 holes are intertwined within a relatively new housing development and the layout is very hacker friendly.

The course gets its name from the many "ponds" that line the course. Calling them ponds might be a bit generous, but swampy areas do abound and you'll find yourself hitting over them more times than you can count. If you have an aversion to hitting over water, this course might cure you of it. The three different nines (red, white, blue) are all relatively the same, but locals claim that the blue and white nines seem to be the most popular.

The course is also very walkable and it has extremely wide fairways, few trees and little elevation changes. It is a links style course wrapped through swamps and meadow and without nasty pocket bunkers. Although walkable, the signage doesn't help matters for the first timer. The tee boxes have small colored markers, but they are painted two different colors so you never know which set of nine you are on. Also, when you play the blue and white nines, they run near each other so you could easily find yourself on the wrong hole. It might be recommended to take a cart the first time just for that reason.

Other than the signage, the course is well maintained, the greens are in great condition, the sand traps well-tended and the asphalt paths, when they are present, are easy to follow. The driving range, found by carting under the highway, is quite average and surprisingly runs alongside one of the holes and could be a potential safety issue with a wicked hook. If you want to start on the red nine, you'll have to cross back through the tunnel to play it.

The clubhouse is very small by today's standards, but they pack in a pro shop, a full bar, a sit-down restaurant area, an event room for parties and a back patio. The space has a nice intimate feel to it like you've just entered the local bar.

THE REFUGE

21250 Yellow Pine Street
Oak Grove, MN 55011
Clubhouse: 763-753-8383
Golf Shop: 763-753-8383
Type: Public   Par: 71
www.refugegolfclub.com

Region: Twin Cities

Course Rating

	HOSPITALITY	8.99
	PLAYABILITY	9.03
P	USABILITY	9.13
U	FACILITY	9.16
F	VALUE	6.69

OVERALL SCORE
883

Tees	Men's	Women's	Yards
Purple		69.4/131	4819
Gold		72.4/139	5372
White	69.7/143	74.9/144	5819
Green	71.4/146		6188
Black	73.0/149		6534

Greens Fee: $41.00 (weekend)
1/2 Cart Fee: $15.00 (weekend)

Reflecting on a summer of golf, most golfers have one course that stands out in his or her mind as the premier golf experience of the season. The course seems to sparkle. The greens are soft and smooth, the fairways perfectly manicured, the sand is fine, the rough is luscious yet playable and the clubhouse is inviting. If this sounds like an ideal golf destination, visit The Refuge Golf Club in Oak Grove, Minnesota.

Oak Grove? Yes, pull out your map. It is worth the drive. Oak Grove is located on Highway 65, approximately 25 miles north of Minneapolis. This sleepy country suburb is home to one of the finest golf courses in the state. This course is carved out of a beautiful, wooded expanse with natural water hazards and boundaries that are as pleasing to the eye as they are challenging to navigate. Although narrow and winding, the fairways call to and guide you through the banks of trees, winding rivers and vast ponds. The sand traps, which pose a threat on nearly half of the holes, are soft like a Caribbean beach. It is truly a remarkable place to golf.

In addition, The Refuge is one of the friendliest courses around. Maybe it is the serene landscape or the relaxed nature of a rural suburb, but everyone is warm, endearing and helpful. The clubhouse attendants and other staff have one purpose in their work: to ensure that each golfer has the most enjoyable golf experience possible. Even one's fellow patrons are patient and eager to offer suggestions about navigating the course. Likewise, the accommodations and amenities are first class. The beautiful clubhouse has a vast banquet facility that is perfect for any event from a wedding to a corporate reception. For golfers, the food is hot and ready on the barbecue for a quick bite at the turn, and the snack and beverage cart appears often to satiate nearly any craving.

Although the course is well managed, its one flaw is in the spacing of golf parties, which leads to congestion on the back nine. Nevertheless, The Refuge is an amazing golf experience that is worth the drive and the slightly higher than average greens fees. Treat yourself, at least once a summer, and find refuge from the panic of city life at The Refuge Golf Club in Oak Grove.

VIKING MEADOWS

1788 Viking Boulevard
Cedar, MN 55011
Clubhouse: 763-434-4205
Golf Shop: 763-434-4205
Type: Public   Par: 72
www.vikingmeadows.com

Course Rating

HOSPITALITY	9.03
PLAYABILITY	8.16
USABILITY	7.75
FACILITY	7.73
VALUE	6.51

OVERALL SCORE
807

Tees	Men's	Women's	Yards
Red		71.2/120	5598
Gold	67.8/117	73.0/124	5745
White	69.9/122		6207
Blue	70.9/124		6428

Greens Fee: $28.00 (weekend)
1/2 Cart Fee: $15.00 (weekend)

NORTHWEST

Very easy to find, Viking Meadows is located only a seven iron east of Highway 65 on Viking Boulevard in East Bethel, Minnesota. The course, marked by ample signage and a long tree-lined drive, brings you to the generous parking lot and clubhouse. Carts are not allowed in the parking lot, so drop your gear in the club drop area or lug it with you. The clubhouse is modest but carries the usual trappings in a compact setting. Fast food, pizza, beverages and a small selection of golf equipment and clothing are there. The front desk is right inside the door and the staff is friendly and accommodating.

The woods may be the first thing you notice once you are on the course. The course has a "Brainerd-like" look with a lot of pines, maples, poplars and birch trees. Outside, between the clubhouse and the first tee, a large display gives you diagrams of all the holes along with 4 sets of yardages. You have a feel for the course before you ever tee it up.

Viking Meadows is a dream course for seniors, juniors, ladies and hackers. There is no stigma for seniors or juniors playing gold tees and the ladies are given ample but fair compensation from the reds. The fairways are generally wide but there are enough hazards to test golfers and to get all of your clubs in play. The course is well maintained and the fairways and greens are in very good condition.

The hazards include sand traps (not a stone to be found in them), water on several holes and a few forest carries over the marshland and creeks that dot the course. The cart paths do not cover the entire course or even continue from tee to green in most cases. However, they are strategically placed and it would be difficult to get lost on this layout. A first-time golfer at Viking Meadows would not have a problem navigating the 18 holes. All in all, intelligent and thoughtful signage and design make this an easy trek for newbies.

Viking Meadows may be lacking in clubhouse amenities but it more than makes up for it in the playability and attractive appearance of the course.

VINTAGE Exec. 18

10444 95th Street NE
Otsego, MN 55362
Clubhouse: 763-271-5000
Golf Shop: 763-271-5000
Type: Public   Par: 58

www.riverwoodnational.com

Tees	Men's	Women's	Yards
Blue	57.2/87	57.7/93	3177

Region: Twin Cities

Course Rating

HOSPITALITY	8.08
PLAYABILITY	7.28
USABILITY	7.45
FACILITY	5.66
VALUE	6.90

OVERALL SCORE
723

Greens Fee: $21.00 (weekend)
1/2 Cart Fee: $ 9.50 (weekend)

Vintage Golf Course, located in Otsego, Minnesota, is an 18-hole executive style golf course located just across the street from its big sister Riverwood National. When you pull into the parking lot just in front of the very small clubhouse, the facilities do not look very impressive. Looks can be deceiving. They definitely are deceiving in this case. Yes, the clubhouse is small but inside you are greeted by warm and friendly staff ready to get you out on the course for your lightning-quick round. The clubhouse has a small bar area, well stocked with drinks, snacks and hot dogs. The pro shop is somewhat limited at Vintage with a few shirts, hats and golf balls but you can stop across the street into the bigger pro shop if you need more apparel.

The course is almost links style with low rolling hills, open fairways and very few if any trees. It is a nice mix of par 3s and 4s with most of the par 3s reachable by a wedge or 9-iron. The par 4s are spaced nicely throughout the course to provide a good test and a needed change of pace during your round. The course is well maintained with very few sand traps and short fairway grass. If you keep the ball in play around the greens you can stay close to par. Vintage is comparable to a links style course in another respect. If you hit your ball into the long grass you will have a difficult time finding it. If you are fortunate enough to locate it in the ankle-high rough you may break your wrists trying to hit it back into play. In combination, the longer grass and well-placed water hazards will steal a couple golf balls and a few strokes from your score. The greens are big enough to provide a good target from the tee box but are soft with very little slope to make for relatively easy putting.

Vintage is a fun course to get out and work on your short iron golf game, which is a weak link for most hackers. Also, finishing your round of golf under the 2.5 hour mark for approximately $20 is refreshing. However, as is the case with most executive style courses, you are left wanting just a little more.

44

WILD MARSH

1710 Montrose Boulevard South
Buffalo, MN 55313
Clubhouse: 763-682-4476
Golf Shop: 763-682-4476 x2
Type: Public   Par: 71
www.wildmarsh.com

Tees	Men's	Women's	Yards
Red		67.3/117	4551
White	67.7/130	72.8/130	5559
Blue	69.8/134	75.5/135	6032
Black	72.0/139		6505

P U

Course Rating

HOSPITALITY	8.99
PLAYABILITY	8.73
USABILITY	9.01
FACILITY	7.96
VALUE	6.73

OVERALL SCORE
854

Greens Fee: $39.00 (weekend)
1/2 Cart Fee: $16.00 (weekend)

NORTHWEST

Wild Marsh Golf Course located in Buffalo, Minnesota, is true to its name. It's an "up north" style course with all the "big city" amenities. A great golf experience is enhanced by the course being very well maintained and a management and staff that take pride in their work.

Located just 25 miles from the intersection of Interstate 494 and Highway 55, Wild Marsh has 18 unique holes. All of the holes are cut through marshes, around lakes and trees, and try to take advantage of the natural rolling terrain. The front nine is more secluded compared to the back nine and snake through residential homes.

With four tee boxes (red – 4551 yards, white – 5559 yards, blue – 6032 yards, and black – 6505 yards) the distance factor off the tee is not a major concern. The course also tries to reach out to the hacker. One advantage that was very helpful was the use of yardage markers. If you are faced with a tee shot that needed to clear a marshy area, a distance marker was embedded at the tee-off. If you do spray off the tee the first cut of rough is cleaned out making it easy to find your ball, but go further into the rough and you'll just have to admit it is a lost ball instead of looking for it in "the bush." The pin placement uses the red (front), white (middle), and blue (back) flags to indicate hole placement on the greens. The greens are nicely sized with some slight dips and slopes.

The course has a great website which will give you all the information you'll need, from seasonal rates to memberships, league play, pro shop deals and the restaurant menu. Also the advantage of booking tee times online is provided through the website.

If you are looking for a peaceful golf experience in a relaxed atmosphere, at the same time being challenged to use every club in your bag, visit Wild Marsh Golf Course in Buffalo, Minnesota.

Twin Cities Courses

NORTHEAST

Applewood Hills	Oneka Ridge
Chomonix	Rush Creek
Gem Lake Hills	Sawmill
Hidden Haven	Stoneridge
Logger's Trail	Tanners Brook
Manitou Ridge	Victory Links
Oak Glen	

COURSE INFO

On June 13, 1991, during the first round of the men's U.S. Open held at Hazeltine National in Chaska, Minnesota, one spectator was killed and five were injured by lightning.

APPLEWOOD HILLS Exec. 18

11840 60th Street North
Stillwater, MN 55082
Clubhouse: 651-439-7276
Golf Shop: 651-439-7276
Type: Public   Par: 62
www.applewoodhillsgolf.com

Region: Twin Cities

H
U

Course Rating

HOSPITALITY	9.45
PLAYABILITY	8.21
USABILITY	9.32
FACILITY	7.96
VALUE	6.58

OVERALL SCORE
854

Tees	Men's	Women's	Yards
Red		59.1/95	3392
White	60.0/98	61.8/102	3891
Blue	60.6/100		4110

Greens Fee: $26.50 (weekend)
1/2 Cart Fee: $15.00 (weekend)

Jobs, kids, yard work, softball, picnics…there are a host of summertime reasons why we may not always have time for a full round of golf. The solution: Applewood Hills Golf Course in Stillwater, Minnesota, an 18-hole, par-62 executive course that is like almost no other in the Twin Cities.   Located just off of Highway 36 at Manning Avenue, Applewood Hills provides a serene, rural setting for a leisurely round of golf on a short but challenging course.

For most golfers, the phrase "executive course" evokes a yawning, defeated response usually accompanied by one of the aforementioned reasons why a full round is untenable. Not so with Applewood Hills. This course is a destination, not a last resort. A beautiful rolling course, lined with blooming apple trees on nearly every fairway, Applewood Hills provides a distinctive golf experience for the beginner and the seasoned golfer alike.

Although Applewood Hills is an executive course, do not leave your driver at home. You will almost certainly need it for the handful of fairways that measure 350 yards or longer. The course layout is relatively imaginative with fairways of varied lengths and shapes, which allows most golfers to play every club in their bag. Even the par-3 holes, which vary in length from 90 to 220 yards, challenge the golfer and provide a demanding "tune-up" for the irons. The greens are likewise varied, from the frustrating "postage-stamp" greens to those that sprawl with entertaining contours. The course is well managed with lush green fairways and ankle-length rough. The only meaningful complaint about this course is a few dead spots on the greens around the curtain. However, even these few dead spots paled in comparison to the overall golf experience.

Applewood Hills is a very walkable course and, at just over $20 per round, very affordable as well. The course also offers league play for men, women, seniors and juniors and twilight rates and enticing internet offers for free or discounted golf. Whether you are short on time, interested in focusing on your short game, or just looking for a break from the menu of your standard courses, Applewood Hills is a great destination.

CHOMONIX

700 Aqua Lane
Lino Lakes, MN 55014
Clubhouse: 651-482-8484
Golf Shop: 651-482-7528
Type: Public   Par: 72

www.chomonix.com

Tees	Men's	Women's	Yards
Red	66.6/117	71.8/124	5445
White	70.8/129		6325
Blue	72.0/131		6596

Course Rating

HOSPITALITY	7.27
PLAYABILITY	6.32
USABILITY	7.54
FACILITY	6.24
VALUE	6.72

OVERALL SCORE
683

Greens Fee: $27.00 (weekend)
1/2 Cart Fee: $13.00 (weekend)

NORTHEAST

A twenty-five minute jog to the northeast of the cities on Interstate 35 will get you to the city of Lino Lakes, Minnesota, where Chomonix Golf Course sits about two miles off the highway.

Part of a regional park reserve, it is clear throughout your round that Chomonix was built into the existing environment. Tall, mature trees constitute the biggest defense against those who spray the ball, while water works its way into play on a very manageable 7 of the 18 holes.

The course does a great job off the bat of giving golfers a chance to build up a head of steam playing the first few tees. Number one plays as a very straightforward and scoreable par 4, which leads into a subtle dogleg par 5 with a very attackable putting surface. If golfers can start out with a couple decent holes, he/she should be able to carry themselves through the rest of the front nine. Golfers can expect whatever number ends up getting posted on that front will increase on the back.

Playing to a total just less than 6600 yards, Chomonix presents itself very fairly as far as distance goes. Eight out of the ten par 4s come in at under 390 yards, and no par 5s are overbearingly long.

As a hacker-friendly course should, the majority of the time, Chomonix offers golfers a safe out for most shots. No 240-yard carries over water can be found, and real estate to the other side of the fairway seems to come more freely when water does come into play.

Bottom line, Chomonix plays like a city course should, and that is right up the alley of an average golfer. Scoring is fair, the prices are right, and the course isn't going to punish any more than you allow it to. As far as getting in your strokes at a comfortable level of play goes, there isn't a whole lot of bad to say about Lino Lakes Chomonix Golf Course.

GEM LAKE HILLS Exec. 18

4039 Scheuneman Road
White Bear Lake, MN 55110
Clubhouse: 651-429-8715
Golf Shop: 651-429-8715
Type: Public   Par: 57

www.gemlakehillsgolf.com

Tees	Men's	Women's	Yards
Red		57.0	2911
White	57.0		3366

Region: Twin Cities

H

Course Rating

HOSPITALITY	9.28
PLAYABILITY	6.05
USABILITY	7.96
FACILITY	5.62
VALUE	6.52

OVERALL SCORE
722

Greens Fee: $22.00 (weekend)
1/2 Cart Fee: $10.00 (weekend)

Gem Lake Hills Golf Course, located in White Bear Lake, Minnesota, is worth the search to find it. It's just east of Highway 61 and County Road F, but you may want to bring your Google map with you since there aren't any local signs directing one to the course. Gem Lake Hills is a great course for beginners, seniors, and those who want to complete a quick 9 or 18 holes. Playing both the par-3 and executive-9 courses is just over 3300 yards and is easily walkable for most golfers. The course offers a number of junior leagues with or without lessons, and there are quite a few adult leagues. The clubhouse doesn't have a pro shop, but it does have friendly, helpful staff along with a good selection of snacks and popcorn.

A large, well-maintained putting and chipping green is close to the clubhouse. Those who wish to warm up at a driving range will have to be satisfied with hitting balls into a large netted area. Since most of the holes average about 170 yards for men, one may want to spend more time on the putting green. Fees are reasonable and the front nine is quite level for those who like to walk. Cold water is available every 2–3 holes, and the beverage cart comes around frequently.

There are few hazards on the course. Golfers encounter one hole where the ball must be driven over a slough, and there are some holes where an errant ball may be lost to water areas. There aren't any sand traps, and trees line some holes, but for the most part trees are only a problem if one drives quite a bit off center or overshoots the green. The fairways and greens are in good condition, while the tee boxes are a bit worn by summer's end. Geese often gather by the 17th and 18th holes.

Most players won't need to use their drivers often at Gem Lake Hills. A decent first shot and a fairly good chip will bring golfers into putting range on the par-3 holes. The cup placement on some of the holes will make achieving a par more difficult than it appears at times. A foursome can easily walk and complete 18 holes in just under four hours on most days. All in all, Gem Lake Hills provides a pleasant golf experience without the challenge of dealing with too many hazards.

HIDDEN HAVEN

20520 NE Polk Street
Cedar, MN 55011
Clubhouse: 763-434-4626
Golf Shop: 763-434-6867
Type: Public   Par: 71

www.hiddenhavengolfclub.com

Tees	Men's	Women's	Yards
Red		68.8/122	4980
White	68.1/125	73.4/131	5806
Blue	68.9/126		5971

Course Rating

H

HOSPITALITY	9.25
PLAYABILITY	7.76
USABILITY	7.54
FACILITY	7.47
VALUE	5.66

OVERALL SCORE
784

Greens Fee: $30.00 (weekend)
1/2 Cart Fee: $14.00 (weekend)

Hidden Haven Golf Club is closer than you think. Located in the North Metro suburb of Cedar, Minnesota, it's just off Highway 65. It's easy to find, and we found it to be true to its namesake—it really is a "hidden haven." Family owned and operated since 1988, it is open to the public. Tee times are handled by calling the course directly. Riding carts are available. There is a smaller pro shop on site, with a fair assortment of accessories and beverages and limited snacks for you at the turn. The main clubhouse, bar, and banquet rooms are located just across the street as you leave the front nine and proceed to the back nine. It was very well attended on this visit and there is a full menu, large bar, pool tables, games, etc. Happy hour drink specials were dirt cheap.

The course itself is well kept, with interesting holes, and landscaped and cared for quite well. There are several homes in close proximity to the course, so being in the fairway is at a premium. We golfed during the morning, so the course was not crowded at all. Check-in was easy and the staff on site was friendly and helpful. The course itself is great for the hacker. A very walkable course at just over 5800 yards from the white tees. Fairly placed greens that are reachable in regulation make it very user friendly for the average golfer. A negative in our minds were a few holes with out-of-bounds stakes too close to the fairways. We found ourselves making what we thought was a relatively good shot only to find as we approached our ball that we were out-of-bounds. Playing the course regularly would help us to avoid those areas. Greens were okay, but had a noticeable difference in cut length and speed from the front nine to the back. Flags on this day were placed fairly, but the greens do have plateaus and provide some challenge so some green reading is necessary.

All in all we enjoyed our day very much, found the course to be one we would enjoy playing again, and to our surprise (for no other reason than ignorance), it really was a hidden gem!

51

LOGGER'S TRAIL

11950 80th Street
Stillwater, MN 55082
Clubhouse: 651-439-7862
Golf Shop: 651-439-7862
Type: Semi-Private   Par: 72

www.sawmillgc.com

Tees	Men's	Women's	Yards
Red		70.7/122	5348
White	68.8/123		6023
Blue	71.7/129		6383
Black	74.5/133		7235

Course Rating

HOSPITALITY   7.43
PLAYABILITY   6.55
USABILITY   7.40
FACILITY   7.09
VALUE   6.20

OVERALL SCORE
699

Greens Fee: $44.00 (weekend)
1/2 Cart Fee: $15.00 (weekend)

NORTHEAST

A visit to Logger's Trail is like a step into the country. Only thirty minutes from downtown St. Paul, it is surrounded by hobby and horse farms and feels more like a course that might be a few hours north. Upon arrival, seeing the links style layout may fool you because it has tight fairways and narrow greens, making this course harder than it looks.

You might think that 6383 yards is a short course , but spend a little time on it and you'll know that if you can't control your ball, it will feel 500 yards longer. The lack of trees may also fool a golfer into thinking that they can spray their tee shots with impunity, but they would be sorely mistaken. Compensating for a lack of natural hazards, the course designers have added numerous strategic bunkers and berms to thwart off-target drives.

The berms are a unique feature, but hitting into them leaves your ball in dry and weedy areas, making recovery shots quite a challenge. Also, hitting out of them makes for blind shots and difficulty assessing distance. The on-course signage is very limited with yardage markers just large discs embedded in the course so expect some searching to determine what club to pull out next.

Playability and challenge are this facility's strengths, but as any hacker knows, there is more to an enjoyable golfing experience than just the course itself and that is where Logger's Trail seems to fall down. The facility's layout is very compact and tightly organized, with only a short walk from the parking lot to the first tee, yet the practice facilities are small and the clubhouse is just a converted trailer.

If you choose to play cart golf, the paths are excellent and nicely integrated into the course. If you are a walker, this course is compact enough that you won't be exhausted by the end of your round. Before your round, though, be warned that the practice putting green is only postage-stamp sized and the driving range requires most golfers to hit over water (we know what hitting over water does for our nerves). Also, food offerings and the pro shop are very limited so stock up before you head out to the first tee.

MANITOU RIDGE

3200 McKnight Road
White Bear Lake, MN 55110
Clubhouse: 651-777-2987
Golf Shop: 651-777-2987 x2
Type: Public   Par: 68
www.manitouridge.com

Tees	Men's	Women's	Yards
Red		71.9/125	5468
White	69.6/123		6034
Blue	71.2/127		6401

Region: Twin Cities

Course Rating

HOSPITALITY	8.22
PLAYABILITY	7.30
USABILITY	7.68
FACILITY	6.35
VALUE	6.71

OVERALL SCORE
740

Greens Fee: $31.00 (weekend)
1/2 Cart Fee: $13.00 (weekend)

NORTHEAST

Manitou is an Algonquian Indian word meaning a supernatural power that controls nature. Fortunately, for those of us golfers classified as hackers, Manitou Ridge Golf Course does not require supernatural intervention to post a respectable score. To the contrary, this rolling wooded course offers a number of challenging holes that allow a hacker to feel good about his game, without the sense of being patronized by straight and mundane fairways.

The most striking aspect of this course, located in White Bear Lake at the intersection of Highway 694 and McKnight Road, is its contoured topography. With rolling fairways, elevated greens and sloped putting surfaces, Manitou Ridge is as beautiful as it is interesting to play. This course uncharacteristically finds the compromise between challenge and playability. The mature tree lines, sharp ridges and other conveniently placed natural hazards enhance the beauty of the course without causing excessive hardship, allowing a player to believe he conquered traps that, in truth, posed no real danger.

In keeping with its non-championship-course designation, Manitou Ridge's predominant downfall is its lack of championship course maintenance. Although the fairways are adequately maintained, its tee boxes, cart paths, roughs and (some) greens leave much to be desired. The roughs are frequently hard and dry, which, for hackers, is bad news, given our propensity to swing from these areas. Unfortunately, these tough spots will account for a few more strokes in your round because the terrain is so unforgiving. The greens are fairly consistent in terms of size and speed, but the imperfect maintenance yields a few frustrating dead spots. To quell your frustrations, Manitou Ridge offers wonderful on-course service, replete with a host of non-alcoholic and alcoholic beverages (including mixed drinks) and a variety of snacks. Likewise, the clubhouse offers a nice selection of potables and edibles at the turn.

Overall, Manitou Ridge is a great course for the value. At $31 per round, this course should be included on your summer golf itinerary.

OAK GLEN

1599 McKusick Road
Stillwater, MN 55082
Clubhouse: 651-439-6981
Golf Shop: 651-439-6963
Type: Public   Par: 72
www.oakglengolf.com

Tees	Men's	Women's	Yards
Red		73.2/134	5626
Gold	69.0/126	74.4/137	5839
White	71.2/131		6320
Blue	72.4/132		6574

Region: Twin Cities

Course Rating

HOSPITALITY   7.88
PLAYABILITY   7.84
USABILITY   8.02
FACILITY   6.86
VALUE   5.91

OVERALL SCORE
755

Greens Fee: $37.00 (weekend)
1/2 Cart Fee: $13.00 (weekend)

Oak Glen Golf Course is a nice find and a reasonable value for what you get. The fairways and greens are very well kept, with nice green grass throughout, even in the middle of a dry Minnesota summer.

The distance plays fairly and, while decent shots are required to hit the greens in regulation, it is certainly an attainable goal for a hacker or average golfer. The rough is not too punishing and the ponds, which are beautiful, are also lateral drops.

The driving range, putting green, and 9-hole par-3 executive course are all located conveniently by the clubhouse.

Our cart, for whatever reason, needed some transmission work, as it kept lurching and had no get-up-and-go. A noticeable amount of the clientele also went out of their way to let us know that this course was their turf, which was interesting. In their defense, they said that Oak Glen was their best-kept local secret and they wanted to keep it that way. Fair enough. We got the hint.

When we made the turn, the single employee behind the register had some problems, to the effect that the marshal actually made a comment to us to hurry up on #10, even though nobody waited on us during the entire back nine.

The cart girl was very friendly and helpful. She took one of our credit cards back to the clubhouse bar to start a tab and then came back to deliver a mixed drink. We saw plenty of her and she came with a decent selection of beverages. A member of our foursome also tipped her to go retrieve a baseball cap that was left two holes back, which she did with a smile.

The course is scenic and the greens are large, forgiving, soft, and consistent.

The website is very informative and helpful. It was very easy to get a tee time, even as late as Friday with a beautiful forecast. If you wanted to spend $50 to play on a Saturday, near the Metro, you should definitely consider hitting Oak Glen.

ONEKA RIDGE

5610 North 12th Street
White Bear Lake, MN 55110
Clubhouse: 651-429-2390
Golf Shop: 651-429-2390
Type: Public   Par: 72

www.onekaridgegc.com

Tees	Men's	Women's	Yards
Red		69.6/117	5166
White	69.7/121	74.6/128	6061
Blue	71.1/126		6360

Course Rating

HOSPITALITY	6.98
PLAYABILITY	7.10
USABILITY	6.80
FACILITY	6.17
VALUE	6.32

OVERALL SCORE
679

Greens Fee: $32.00 (weekend)
1/2 Cart Fee: $14.00 (weekend)

NORTHEAST

Located in White Bear Lake, Minnesota, Oneka Ridge Golf Course plays to 6061 yards. The website claims a practice green with a practice bunker, but this reviewer did not see the bunker anywhere. The one practice green that was found near the first hole was a decent size with no holes cut in it, just the little stick-in flags.

The range was a little bit away from the clubhouse and you had to pass by #10 and #14 to get to it. It's on the small size with only about 7 stalls. There were 3 target "greens" on the range that were actually just sand hills.

Tee boxes are in fine shape. One nice feature is that each hole has an aerial photo showing the entire hole with landing areas marked out with distances. Fairways are in pretty good condition, not overly wide or too small either.

Greens are in fine shape with your typical 4–5 pitch marks per green but they rolled decently once they dried up from the morning dew. Greens were mostly sized medium-large and fairly flat with some character.

Overall flow of the course was decent and you could easily find your next hole. Signage wasn't that necessary since the green you just played and the next box are a very short distance apart. One major complaint is that the course "feels" tight. It's not the individual holes themselves that are tight, quite the contrary. It's the way they have this course laid out that makes you feel you are on top of other holes around you. If you are having a bad day with the sticks, you could easily be hitting into other tee boxes or other greens.

The clubhouse is on the smallish side but has inside and outside seating areas to rest after the round. Food selection is inexpensive, but is very typical microwaveable fare. One nice feature for those who like to forget things like scorecards is that you can get one from the pro shop which you pass a million times, or on #2 and #11. This is a scoreable course with few trouble spots so your score shouldn't suffer, but don't expect much in the way of amenities.

RUSH CREEK

7801 Troy Lane
Maple Grove, MN 55311
Clubhouse: 763-494-0400
Golf Shop: 763-494-8844
Type: Public   Par: 72

www.rushcreek.com

F

Course Rating

HOSPITALITY	9.01
PLAYABILITY	8.61
USABILITY	7.82
FACILITY	8.56
VALUE	5.98

OVERALL SCORE
828

Tees	Men's	Women's	Yards
Green		72.0/131	5317
Silver	71.3/137	77.2/141	6204
Blue	73.2/140	79.4/146	6747
Gold	74.8/144		7117

Greens Fee: $105.00 (weekend)
1/2 Cart Fee: $19.00 (weekend)

NORTHEAST

We are tempted to write a one sentence review about Rush Creek Golf Club in Maple Grove, Minnesota. The place is simply exquisite. Ok, we'll write more but be warned, typed words won't do this course justice.

We rolled into the parking lot early one Friday morning and were immediately greeted by a very nice gentleman who took our bags and set them up for us on a cart. We got there early before the round to work some kinks out. The course has an expansive area to warm up, from an enormous practice green to a driving range with a full set of slots. (Side note: if we had to come up with a complaint about Rush Creek it would be that the driving range faces dead towards the rising sun in the morning so it is hard at times to track your ball.)

The course itself is lush. Fairways almost seem to be divot-free and the rough is not incredibly difficult to get out from. The greens were large and in perfect shape. This could be due to the fact that the starter gave us each a tool to replace ball marks in the greens.

Water does come into play on a good number of holes as the entire course seems to be intertwined with a creek-like area (perhaps that is why they call it Rush Creek) but don't let it get in your head. On most holes you can clear it with little trouble.

The par 3s are a reasonable distance, all around 150–160 yards, and the par 5s provide a good chance to score well. Hole #13 is a classic, forcing you to go over water twice. The shots you need to hit are not very hard but that water looms in your head like a bad dream.

Service at Rush Creek is phenomenal. Everywhere you turn the staff is there and willing to help to make your time on the golf course the best time of your day.

When you're done with your round, take an opportunity to enjoy the beautiful porch of the clubhouse decked out with comfortable furniture and fire pits. Drinks and a full menu are served on the patio so eat up.

SAWMILL

11177 North McKusick Road
Stillwater, MN 55082
Clubhouse: 651-439-7862 x2
Golf Shop: 651-439-7862 x2
Type: Semi-Private   Par: 70

www.sawmillgc.com

Tees	Men's	Women's	Yards
Red		68.5/124	4891
White	67.3/118	71.8/131	5470
Blue	68.6/121	73.5/134	5766
Black	71.2/123		6238

Course Rating

HOSPITALITY	8.61
PLAYABILITY	8.04
USABILITY	8.18
FACILITY	6.28
VALUE	7.20

OVERALL SCORE
786

Greens Fee: $28.00 (weekend)
1/2 Cart Fee: $15.00 (weekend)

NORTHEAST

Sawmill Golf Course is tucked away in the woods about 5 miles off of Highway 36 in Stillwater, Minnesota, and if you have any desire to score well, you may want to tuck away that driver on about seven of the holes.

At their current rates, $28 for 18 holes, this course has to be the best hole-for-hole deal in the Metro area. The beauty and challenge of the 150-yard par-3 fifth hole is worth four bucks alone. You tee off straight over a monster pond that has to eat golf balls like Kobayashi eats Nathan's hot dogs, but it's not that tough a hole if you can put the water out of your head.

Several of the longer holes that require a driver are tree lined and picturesque but don't try to kill that drive or you may just need a chainsaw to find it in the wood. The opening par 5 is a pretty simple hole and can be a confidence booster if you par it. The course has great terrain as several of the holes go up and down hill. The only complaint is that the fairways were rather wet—likely attributable to the previous night's rain and not overwatering by the grounds crew.

Get to the course early and there are several areas to help you warm up. Plenty of room in the parking lot allows for a quick stretch before you reach the clubhouse where you'll find three chipping and putting areas. Buy a bucket of balls and you can hit the driver off the range about 30 yards from the first tee.

Staff on the course are fantastic and we even had a chance to shoot the breeze with course designer Dan Pohl after the round. The clubhouse, while situated perfectly, is nothing to write home about but it does suffice for a place to grab a quick bite and pay for your round.

Lastly, you may hear rumors swirling that this course is set for demolition so that a condo community can be built. That is not the case—at least not for another five years. So, get to the course, grab those twenties out of your wallet and get out on this short, yet challenging track. And leave the money you save with the staff— they deserve it.

STONERIDGE

13600 North Hudson Boulevard
Stillwater, MN 55082
Clubhouse: 651-436-4653
Golf Shop: 651-436-4653 x4
Type: Semi-Private   Par: 72

www.stoneridgegc.com

Tees	Men's	Women's	Yards
Green		70.7/126	5247
White	70.2/134	75.6/136	6131
Blue	72.8/139		6702
Black	74.2/142		6992

Region: Twin Cities

Course Rating

HOSPITALITY   8.23
PLAYABILITY   7.65
USABILITY   6.35
FACILITY   7.69
VALUE   6.03

OVERALL SCORE
738

Greens Fee: $79.00 (weekend)
1/2 Cart Fee: $26.00 (weekend)

Stoneridge Golf Club in Stillwater, Minnesota, is located adjacent to Interstate 94 and very close to the Minnesota/Wisconsin border. It is a links style course, reminiscent of the courses of Scotland and Ireland. This course mimics a golf purist's vision of a "real golf course." It has been regarded in some venues as being "one of the best public courses in Minnesota."

Upon our arrival we were met in the parking lot by attendants on carts who asked to take our clubs and have them ready for us after check-in. We walked into the large clubhouse to check in and were greeted by name. They gave us information about the course, and a free ball repair tool to use with their repair system. We were offered bottled water gratis, and also a bucket of balls to hit before our round. There is a driving range and practice green close to the first hole. Our clubs were ready and waiting for us as we boarded our cart and started our round.

This is a very difficult course, with undulating fairways and greens and peppered with expansive and/or deep bunkers on nearly every hole. Playing to about 6150 yards from the white tees, it is imperative that you are in the fairway on your drives or on the greens in regulation to have any chance at a par.

If you are a very low handicap player and feel the need to find new challenges, this course is for you. For the mid-teen on up handicap player, this most likely will not be an enjoyable experience for you. There is little landscaping on the course in keeping with the links style. One thing we found that we did not like was the fact that the cart paths often left us quite a distance from the greens. We were continually parking the cart and grabbing a couple clubs, or more, and heading off to our ball. After our round, attendants were there to greet us again, providing assistance if we needed it.

The folks at Stoneridge were very personable and accommodating—we could not have asked for more. Unfortunately, we were there for the golf, and to look for the hacker-friendly aspects in our round, and we found them few and far between on this day.

TANNERS BROOK

5810 190th Street
Forest Lake, MN 55025
Clubhouse: 651-464-2300
Golf Shop: 651-464-2300
Type: Public   Par: 71
www.tannersbrook.com

V

Course Rating

HOSPITALITY	8.63
PLAYABILITY	7.20
USABILITY	6.88
FACILITY	6.93
VALUE	7.62

OVERALL SCORE
749

Greens Fee: $33.00 (weekend)
1/2 Cart Fee: $14.00 (weekend)

Tees	Men's	Women's	Yards
Red		70.9/124	5332
Gold	67.9/124	73.2/129	5753
White	70.3/127	76.3/135	6283
Blue	72.4/129		6691
Black	73.3/130		6887

NORTHEAST

Tanners Brook Golf Course in Forest Lake, Minnesota, provides what you could call a hacker's dream. Imagine tall prairie grass as far as the eye could see; a picturesque site with wide fairways and rough plenty far out of reach. This is then coupled with short fast fairways and very receptive greens that brings the distance on the scorecard down to a manageable length for the everyday hacker.

Tanners Brook's clubhouse is a subtle structure from the outside but warm and welcoming on the interior. Set in a farm landscape and nestled right next to an old barn, it creates a very interesting composition. Adjacent to the clubhouse is a practice green and a driving area. There is also a nice putting green located right behind the first tee, so you may continue to warm up while you are waiting to tee off.

The first tee is not very well marked since it is across the parking lot and the road. When we were looking for the first tee the staff was gracious to help us and even gave us a ride to the first tee, which was well appreciated.

The course offers quite a variety of total distances and even from the tips the course is quite reasonable because of the hard, fast, and wide-open fairways. Hitting from these fairways into the greens is a joy. The greens are not only receptive to iron shots, they also roll with a good pace and are very true. The par 5s are reachable with a couple of good hits, but through the use of water and bunkers there is some risk and reward involved. One complaint about the course is the par 3s—while they are nice holes, they seemed a bit long and would have been much more enjoyable a club or two shorter in length. Besides the long walk to the #1 and #10 tee boxes, the course was enjoyable to walk. The holes where well spaced without creating long walks from tee to green.

Overall this is a good course for the everyday hacker, greens fees are reasonable and the course is well maintained. What it may lack in memorable signature holes it makes up for in enjoyment and playability, which is why we play golf in the first place, right?

VICTORY LINKS

1700 105th Avenue NE
Blaine, MN 55449
Clubhouse: 763-717-3240
Golf Shop: 763-717-3240
Type: Public   Par: 71
www.golfnygc.org

Region: Twin Cities

Course Rating

HOSPITALITY	6.83
PLAYABILITY	6.25
USABILITY	7.09
FACILITY	6.95
VALUE	5.68

Tees	Men's	Women's	Yards
Flagstone	62.8/115	66.1/113	4475
Bronze	63.9/118	68.1/118	4848
Silver	67.2/124	72.1/126	5560
Gold	70.5/131	76.1/134	6282
Iron	74.7/135		7092

OVERALL SCORE
661

Greens Fee: $42.00 (weekend)
1/2 Cart Fee: $14.00 (weekend)

The full name of the course is Victory Links at the National Youth Golf Center and is part of the National Sports Center in Blaine, Minnesota. It is a very pleasant and well thought out course. Golf course staff are friendly and helpful. Several holes offer very aesthetically appealing views. It is a relatively level course that is easy to walk and when visited, the fairways and greens were in tournament condition. With the exception of the noise from planes taking off at the Anoka County Airport (next door) which is surprisingly busy, the holes are well screened from the road and traffic noise and sight lines, which gives the golfer the feeling of a rural golf course in the heart of a major metro area.

This course is fundamentally designed to develop the young golfer. There are multiple tee boxes on each hole to relate to the golfer's ability. The course ranges from 2834 yards (for juniors) to 7100 yards depending on the golfer's tee box selection. Several lesson plans are available through the pro shop targeted towards youth development.

A unique concept of this course is the 18-hole putting course. Time permitting, you may want to avail yourself of this amenity before your round of golf. A keen putting eye is important on this course as the greens are tricky and the cups unforgiving. Fellow hackers will find that hitting the center of the cup is necessary to ensure a drop.

Facilities are lacking in some regards. There are no restaurant facilities but there is a hot dog stand and beverage cart. Women golfers might want to bring along some extra Kleenex as the only restrooms are at the clubhouse and porta-potties are few and far between.

While Victory Links is not the cheapest course around it is a very pretty course that offers as much challenge as you may desire. Be warned though, it has the longest walk to the first tee of any course in the Twin Cities, but once you get there, the starter is quite a friendly fellow.

NORTHEAST

60

Twin Cities Courses

Baker National	Hiawatha
Bluff Creek	Hyland Greens
Boulder Pointe	Lakeview
Braemar	Legends
Brookview	Meadowbrook
Chaska Town	Pioneer Creek
Columbia	Ridges at Sand Creek
Crystal Lake	Stonebrooke
Dahlgreen	The Meadows
Deer Run	The Wilds
Dwan	Theodore Wirth
Fox Hollow	Timber Creek
Francis A. Gross	Valley View
Heritage Links	

Cragun's Legacy Courses in Brainerd were only the second resort course in the world to be designated an Audubon International Signature Sanctuary (the first being Pinehurst in North Carolina).

BAKER NATIONAL

2935 Parkview Drive
Medina, MN 55340
Clubhouse: 763-694-7670
Golf Shop: 763-694-7670
Type: Public   Par: 72

www.bakernational.com

Tees	Men's	Women's	Yards
Yellow		72.0/131	5313
White	71.8/131	77.5/142	6294
Black	73.9/135		6762

Region: Twin Cities

Course Rating

HOSPITALITY	8.68
PLAYABILITY	8.53
USABILITY	7.67
FACILITY	8.17
VALUE	7.42

V

OVERALL SCORE
823

Greens Fee: $36.00 (weekend)
1/2 Cart Fee: $15.00 (weekend)

Baker National Golf Course in Medina, Minnesota, is located within the Three Rivers Park District and is the hacker's dream setting. With an expansive practice area, a championship 18-hole course, an executive 9-hole course and a well-stocked clubhouse, you can spend your chosen amount of time leisurely perfecting your golf game.

The course entrance and clubhouse (pro shop) were easy to find even though it is set back off of any highway, but that does mean no car noises to distract you. The pro shop is well stocked, and the staff were very pleasant and helpful. They eagerly checked our foursome in and directed us to the practice ranges and putting greens. Yes, practice ranges and putting greens.

When warmed up we hopped into the electric carts and drove them to the first tee. Although the course can be walked, the rolling fairways will test your stamina and on the back nine some "next tees" are a good walk away from the last hole's green. The nice lady starter checked our time and wished us good luck.

The championship course was very lush and the setting could not be more picturesque. The fairways were a tad narrow but the rough was not very punishing. Plus on the front nine, we found out first hand, you can spray your drive and still find your ball in a playable lie. The back nine holes are tighter and you do need to play some position golf rather than just "grip it and rip it" all the time. What was nice to see was that every sprinkler head did have a yardage marker on it and the 150-yard marker was very visible. All of the greens challenged our putting skills as the greens all seemed to have two or three tiers. The greens are large in size; hence it built up our self-esteem when we landed on from outside 150 yards. The pace of play for a Sunday was average, just over 4½ hours for the round, but we did see the beverage cart every three holes.

Overall, Baker National Golf Course is a hacker's dream setting and we would definitely make a return trip each summer.

SOUTHWEST

62

BLUFF CREEK

1025 Creekwood
Chaska, MN 55318
Clubhouse: 952-445-5685
Golf Shop: 952-445-5685
Type: Public   Par: 72
www.bluffcreek.com

Tees	Men's	Women's	Yards
Red		71.1/125	5629
White	71.0/122	76.7/137	6398
Blue	71.9/124		6641

Course Rating

HOSPITALITY	7.86
PLAYABILITY	6.96
USABILITY	6.86
FACILITY	6.95
VALUE	5.42

OVERALL SCORE
700

Greens Fee: $42.00 (weekend)
1/2 Cart Fee: $15.00 (weekend)

Bluff Creek Golf Course in Chanhassen, Minnesota, might be considered a hidden gem and it tries hard to stay that way. If you didn't know it was there you'd miss it. If you are lucky enough to find the sign and do make the turn, you'll drive along what appears like a residential blacktop and even when you pull into the parking lot, you'll have to walk right up to the building to make sure you are at the right place.

Once there, you might be fooled when seeing the clubhouse for the first time. It is quite plain and doesn't hint at the airy, modern interior. After checking in, you find your cart just outside the door, the driving range nearby and a nice undulating putting green that will foreshadow the greens you'll find on the course.

The course itself is beautifully situated in the rolling hills and colorful hardwoods of Chanhassen. It is not really a walker's course because of the significant elevation changes. Although the holes are fairly straight with wide fairways, the greens don't do a golfer any favors because of the undulations. If you are not careful, they could easily add 4 to 5 strokes to your score. You won't find a lot of water, but you'll have to hone your sand skills because bunkers are often strategically tucked around the greens.

The course's strong suit is its setting, especially later in the year. It is a good course for hackers with equal opportunities for risk/reward and an average golfer has a chance to score well. Where it seems weak is the cost/value because the pricing seems a bit high for what you get and with its remote location you don't have many food/drink options nearby and are stuck with standard course fare.

If you are looking for a fair test, Bluff Creek is the kind of course that is good for the average player. If you are looking for a place to celebrate after your round, be sure to stop by Lion's Tap on Flying Cloud Drive, only a two-mile drive from the course. It is known for serving some of the best burgers in the Twin Cities.

SOUTHWEST

BOULDER POINTE

9575 Glenborough Drive
Elko, MN 55020
Clubhouse: 952-461-4900
Golf Shop: 952-461-4900
Type: Public   Par: 71

www.boulderpointegolf.com

Tees	Men's	Women's	Yards
Red	64.7/118	69.0/122	4794
Gold	67.6/123	72.5/129	5426
White	69.5/126		5833
Black	71.2/131		6224

Course Rating

HOSPITALITY	6.12
PLAYABILITY	7.50
USABILITY	7.35
FACILITY	7.01
VALUE	6.15

OVERALL SCORE
692

Greens Fee: $34.00 (weekend)
1/2 Cart Fee: $15.00 (weekend)

Boulder Pointe Golf Club, located in Elko, Minnesota, a couple miles west of Interstate 35W, is a very picturesque course with nice elevation changes and lots of great scenery. If you hit the ball well and keep it in play this can be an enjoyable course. However, if you have a tendency to spray your ball a little bit or slice or hook it, you could be in for a long afternoon.

Generally speaking, the course was in excellent shape, with the exception of a few of the tee boxes that needed a little work. The fairways were nice and the rough was not too difficult to play out of. The greens played very true, although with lots of undulations they can be quite tricky. This is definitely a golf course that calls for course management. Club selection is the key. For the first timer this course can cause some problems. Lots of hazards and trouble to get into here.

One thing that was especially helpful was the GPS on all the golf carts. This made club selection much easier. Another nice feature of the GPS was that it showed where the group ahead of you was, and how far away they were (nice feature for those of us who may have a tendency of not knowing if we can hit away).

Boulder Pointe also had a great clubhouse. It has a nice little pro shop with an assortment of balls, clubs, shoes, and apparel. It also has a very nice restaurant that serves appetizers, soups, salads, burgers, sandwiches, pastas, and pizza. There is also a full bar serving mixed drinks, tap and bottle beer, and wine.

One of the greatest things about this course was its staff. Very friendly, professional, and genuinely interested in your having a good time. In particular was one young man working in the pro shop. As we were about to leave, our friend must have left his lights on and so his car would not start. The man behind the counter offered to give us a jump, and we were soon on our way.

All in all, our group enjoyed our golf outing at Boulder Pointe. It is certainly not the easiest course to play, but if you are up for a challenge, want to see a beautiful course, and enjoy a nice day of golf, we would recommend this one.

SOUTHWEST

BRAEMAR

6364 John Harris Drive
Edina, MN 55439
Clubhouse: 952-826-6791
Golf Shop: 952-826-6799
Type: Public   Par: 36/36/36

www.braemargolf.com

Tees	Men's	Women's	Yards
Castle/Hays - Red	67.5/118	73.1/126	5702
Castle/Hays - White	70.4/124	76.7/133	6341
Hays/Clunie - Red	66.3/117	71.6/122	5706
Hays/Clunie - White	69.1/123	75.0/129	5972
Clunie/Castle - Red	67.5/121	73.0/128	5579
Clunie/Castle - White	71.2/129	77.6/137	6401

Course Rating

HOSPITALITY	9.31
PLAYABILITY	8.58
USABILITY	8.74
FACILITY	8.99
VALUE	6.96

H
F

OVERALL SCORE
869

Greens Fee: $36.00 (weekend)
1/2 Cart Fee: $16.00 (weekend)

Braemar Golf Course is owned and operated by the City of Edina, Minnesota, and features 27 regulation holes, a 9-hole executive course, banquet facilities, meeting rooms, and a grill that serves breakfast, sandwiches, beer and wine.

Braemar is probably the most unique and diverse course in the Twin Cities area. It has hosted PGA Tour events, amateur championships, numerous Minnesota Golf Association tournaments; has men's leagues, junior golf leagues, 12 women's leagues; and the Sister Kenny Institute holds a golf league for golfers with disabilities. Braemar also is a member of the Cooperative Sanctuary Program of Audubon International. The driving range is probably the heaviest used range in the Twin Cities. Next to the driving range is a large putting green that you can putt or chip.

The front nine (Castle 1-9) is the longest of the three courses. We would recommend the red tees for mid to high handicaps as there are four holes over 400 yards from the white tees. The second nine (Hays 10-18) has a more interesting terrain than the Castle and is also relatively flat except the par-3 #12 with the tee near the top of a hill. The Castle and Hays nines are the original 18 holes. Their fairways are generous in width, the greens moderately undulating, quite large and in excellent condition. They are also well bunkered, but there is often an opening to run the ball up.

The third nine (Clunie 19-27) is the newest course. The Minnesota Department of Natural Resources (DNR) had significant input on this course's design as it wanders through a number of natural hazards and dense wooded areas. Clunie might be too difficult for the higher handicap player. Others will find it fun and challenging. Clunie is much more difficult to walk as there are three long uphill climbs from green to tee. The condition of Clunie was similar to the original course except the fairways weren't in quite as good condition with some bare spots.

Centrally located, Braemer is a very busy place that is well managed, well maintained and has everything you would want from a full-service golf course.

SOUTHWEST

BROOKVIEW

200 Brookview Parkway
Golden Valley, MN 55426
Clubhouse: 763-512-2300
Golf Shop: 763-512-2330
Type: Public   Par: 72

www.brookviewgolf.com

Tees	Men's	Women's	Yards
Red		71.1/122	5328
Gold	67.1/123	72.4/125	5569
White	69.6/129	75.5/131	6123
Blue	70.8/131		6387

Region: Twin Cities

Course Rating

HOSPITALITY	8.53
PLAYABILITY	7.36
USABILITY	8.03
FACILITY	7.02
VALUE	6.53

OVERALL SCORE
765

Greens Fee: $34.00 (weekend)
1/2 Cart Fee: $14.00 (weekend)

Brookview Golf Course is in the heart of Golden Valley, Minnesota, and because of its location, is one of the busiest courses in the Twin Cities. Just off of Highway 55, it has an irons-only driving range, a par-3 course and 18 holes of urban golf.

With more than 40,000 rounds played yearly, the course has a large staff to keep the course in good condition. Although it doesn't have many bunkers or man-made hazards, there are just enough water and woods obstacles to make the course more challenging than it appears.

The clubhouse is comfortable with a lot of windows and a nice grill that serves both breakfast and lunch fare. The pricing is reasonable and the service is quick. Golden Valley city rules don't allow for more than beer and wine. Another thing to consider is that the course is smoke free.

Brookview is walkable with some elevation changes. Many of the holes are pretty flat, but water and swampy areas do come into play with certain holes requiring a layup. One weakness that often is found at similar courses is signage and the course can use a little help here. Directional signage to point you to the next hole and distance markers are sometimes hard to see. If you've played the course before it shouldn't be a big problem, but if it is your first time then you might pull out the wrong club or make the wrong turn.

The course has just enough challenge for hackers so don't be surprised by the loss of a few balls during your round. For a city course Brookview holds up well. It doesn't have the cachet of fancier courses, but it provides enough risk/reward that an average player has chances to score well.

For those in the city, Brookview is priced reasonably for a weekend round, and you don't have an hour of driving time to get there. If you want to warm up your driver, the range's lawyers won't let you do that because you might bean someone driving along Highway 55. If you want the 19th hole, the Brookview Grill is nice, but there are a number of nicer watering holes nearby.

CHASKA TOWN

3000 Town Course Drive
Chaska, MN 55318
Clubhouse: 952-443-3748
Golf Shop: 952-443-3748
Type: Public   Par: 72

www.chaskatowncourse.com

Tees	Men's	Women's	Yards
Red		69.4/119	4853
Red/White		71.6/124	5246
White	70.0/132	75.6/132	6038
Green	71.9/136	78.0/137	6397
Green/Black	72.5/137		6531
Black	73.8/140		6817

Course Rating

HOSPITALITY	9.08
PLAYABILITY	8.85
USABILITY	9.19
FACILITY	8.73
VALUE	5.88

H
P
U
F

OVERALL SCORE
866

Greens Fee: $58.00 (weekend)
1/2 Cart Fee: $16.00 (weekend)

The Chaska Town Course is owned and operated by the City in Chaska, Minnesota. There are four sets of tees ranging from 4853 yards to 6817 yards. Chaska has done something unique in that the scorecard shows six different distances. In addition to the four tees, they have a black/green distance which is a combination of the two longest tees. At the other end of the spectrum is the red/white distance which is a combination of the two shortest tees.

We found the secret was to pick the correct tees. We chose the white tees at 6038 yards which had a course rating of 70.0 and a slope of 132. It turned out to be the correct choice and it provided a good challenge and an enjoyable round.

The fairways were all very generous in their width. The rough was a consistent two inches, the bunkers were the best we've played, but the greens had a number of ball mark bruises that didn't heal very well.

The front nine was interesting as you went from a 408-yard second hole to the third hole of 254 yards with a big tree in the middle of the fairway about 50 yards from the green. The back nine was the tougher of the two with #11 at 410 yards the toughest hole on the course. After your drive you have to negotiate trees on the right and a pond on the left that ran up to the green. The course layout is excellent with the cart paths and signage very good. There was water available every other hole and more restrooms than any course we've played. The golf carts were unique in that the GPS was built into the dashboard. The practice area is first class and in wonderful shape.

The clubhouse is average size with a nice pro shop, a friendly staff, and the Chaska Town Course Grille that has the usual menu and bar. The Grille seating area is a little small and can probably seat 50 to 75 people.

Chaska Town Course will give you an upscale experience at half the cost where golfers of all skills can have an enjoyable experience.

SOUTHWEST

COLUMBIA

3300 Central Avenue NE
Minneapolis, MN 55418
Clubhouse: 612-789-2627
Golf Shop: 612-789-2627
Type: Public   Par: 71

www.minneapolisparks.org

Tees	Men's	Women's	Yards
Red		69.8/121	5152
White	69.5/122	75.2/132	6121
Blue	70.6/124		6371

Region: Twin Cities

Course Rating

HOSPITALITY	7.74
PLAYABILITY	7.44
USABILITY	6.50
FACILITY	5.59
VALUE	5.69

OVERALL SCORE
688

Greens Fee: $30.00 (weekend)
1/2 Cart Fee: $14.00 (weekend)

Columbia Golf Course, located in northeast Minneapolis, is actually the second oldest course in the Minneapolis park system. Founded in 1919, it has evolved over the years and continues to be a very busy and popular golf course. At 6371 yards from the tips, it is well within the capabilities of most golfers.

Shoehorned by the city, the course tries to overcome its limited length with mature trees, strategically placed bunkers, hazards and changing elevations. On certain holes, hitting into the side of a hill isn't necessarily a bad thing. Although very compact, there are still some decent walks that must be made between a few holes, reminding you that you should have rented a cart.

The clubhouse has a country club feel with a small pro shop and a nice eating area with flat screen TVs. The facility is nicely organized with parking only a short distance from the first tee. One major drawback is that although they have a nice practice center (Columbia Driving Range), it is not within walking distance and is situated on the opposite side of the course. A golfer who wanted to hit a few balls before his round would need to add at least 30 minutes to his day.

Unlike many overly busy urban courses, the staff, from the food counter to the starter, were all very pleasant and efficient. Where the course seemed to need some help was maintenance. Although the day the course was rated the weather had been dry, the course seemed to have a number of fairways and a couple of greens with brown or dead spots. This could be partially attributed to the weather, but other courses rated at the same time didn't seem to have this problem so it doesn't appear that this is the only reason.

For the average golfer, you can't beat the value. At $30, you can play this urban course and not have to make an hour's drive to get there. The course seems to mirror its working-class urban location, so if you are looking for a fancy, well-manicured track, this isn't your course. If you are looking for a chance to score well where the staff is pleasant, the course should give you a shot at lowering your score.

SOUTHWEST

CRYSTAL LAKE

16725 Innsbrook Drive
Lakeville, MN 55044
Clubhouse: 952-432-6566
Golf Shop: 952-432-6566
Type: Public   Par: 71

www.crystallakegolfcourse.com

Tees	Men's	Women's	Yards
Front	64.0/118	68.3/119	4805
Middle	68.7/127	74.0/131	5825
Back	70.8/132		6306

F

Course Rating

HOSPITALITY   8.41
PLAYABILITY   8.35
USABILITY   7.88
FACILITY   9.01
VALUE   6.76

OVERALL SCORE
821

Greens Fee: $40.00 (weekend)
1/2 Cart Fee: $15.00 (weekend)

Crystal Lake Golf Course is located in Lakeville, Minnesota, and is a tale of two different nines. The front nine rambles through a residential area with gentle rolling hills. The back nine is flat and meanders among natural wetlands. The course is walkable but the front nine has a number of medium to long walks between greens and tees. The walk from the first green to the second tee and the eighth green to the ninth tee requires a walk over a street bridge.

The clubhouse has a pro shop, banquet facilities, and snack shop with a variety of food choices, beer and even cigars. It is small and compact, but well stocked, very friendly and helpful. There is also a nice patio overlooking the driving range. The driving range is in back of the clubhouse and very spartan. The tee area grass is barely adequate and the range consists of a field bordered by wetlands and no flags or distance markers. The putting green was large and rolling and in excellent condition.

We found all aspects of the course in excellent condition. The greens had been aerated a couple of weeks previous, but were smooth and much faster than the putting green. The greens were undulated and most tilted back to front which made putting very difficult in any position other than directly below the hole. The rough was about two inches high, but the ball would settle down and was difficult to find and even more difficult to hit a quality shot. The cart paths are a combination of blacktop, concrete and gravel and are well routed around the course. The golf carts are electric with GPS. We weren't impressed with the GPS as it displayed ads between each hole and most of the time you had to manually press the buttons to get to the next hole. The distances in the GPS to the green were to the front and the center, not to the flag.

Even though the course was in excellent condition the overall golfing experience didn't excite us. Some holes seem a bit ill-conceived with blind approaches to the green, and for hackers wary of water, there are three holes with carries of 90 to 125 yards over wetlands.

DAHLGREEN

6940 Dahlgreen Road
Chaska, MN 55318
Clubhouse: 952-448-7463
Golf Shop: 952-448-7463
Type: Semi-Private   Par: 72

www.dahlgreen.com

Tees	Men's	Women's	Yards
Red		69.9/126	5108
Gold	69.3/128	73.9/135	5831
White	72.4/134	77.8/143	6527
Blue	73.5/136		6761

Region: Twin Cities

Course Rating

HOSPITALITY	8.41
PLAYABILITY	7.14
USABILITY	7.71
FACILITY	7.30
VALUE	6.43

OVERALL SCORE
753

Greens Fee: $42.00 (weekend)
1/2 Cart Fee: $15.00 (weekend)

If you look on a map, you might think that Dahlgreen Golf Club really doesn't exist because the course claims it is located in Chaska, Minnesota. Yet, it is there right off Highway 212 with a Chaska address. Everything about Dahlgreen is big: the parking lot, the fairways, and the greens. Surrounded by farms, the course is like a visit to the country and if the wind is blowing in the right direction, you'll know that a dairy farm is just next door.

With the completion of Highway 212 a few years ago, the time to get to the course has been shortened by at least 15 minutes for those coming from the Twin Cities. To give you an additional reason to visit, the course offers a 50-cents/mile discount (up to 30 miles) if you are coming to the course. That is usually equivalent to a free cart.

The course first opened in 1968 and has grown to become a sprawling 6761 yards with broad fairways and large gradually sloped greens. Although large, these greens are also very fast so you will have to have a light touch to find the hole. Course hole signage is good with a picture of the hole just under the listed yardages, but the on-course distance markers only show the 150-yard marks with other distances difficult to find. If you are taking a cart, your distance worries will be for naught because they have a very simple GPS system that is easy to use and doesn't block the cart windshield.

The course's only real weakness is that it ends with a par-4 final hole that has an awful approach onto an elevated green. That might not be bad, but it probably has at least a 100-foot elevation change and if you hit to the right you'll find your ball down a very steep hill and will need mountaineering gear to get up and down.

The clubhouse is a bit dated with 1970s era paneling, but it does have a nice bar and the Willows Bar & Restaurant is an inexpensive stop for the 19th hole. If you're on your way to Mankato or St. Peter, consider Dahlgreen on your way out of town.

DEER RUN

8661 Deer Run Drive
Victoria, MN 55386
Clubhouse: 952-443-2351
Golf Shop: 952-443-2351
Type: Semi-Private   Par: 71
www.deerrungolf.com

Course Rating

H
F

HOSPITALITY	9.38
PLAYABILITY	8.61
USABILITY	8.63
FACILITY	8.98
VALUE	7.01

OVERALL SCORE
871

Tees	Men's	Women's	Yards
Red		69.3/118	5040
Gold	65.9/118	70.6/120	5273
White	69.8/126	75.5/131	6146
Black	70.5/128		6292

Greens Fee: $54.00 (weekend)
1/2 Cart Fee: $15.00 (weekend)

If you are tired of playing a round that seems to take hours at your local course, you might want to try to book a tee time on a "Fast Play Friday" at Deer Run Golf Club located in Victoria, Minnesota. On "Fast Play Fridays" if your group doesn't finish the front nine in the required 1 hour and 55 minutes you are given a rain check and asked to leave the course. The starters and rangers are present and watchful, but not intrusive. On the Friday that we played, this policy made for a very pleasant round that did not feel rushed or hurried. The policy alone might be enough to recommend Deer Run; however, there is much more to this course than a fast round.

Deer Run is a beautiful and extremely well-maintained course set amidst lovely homes in the western suburbs. The condition of the course was ideal with lush green fairways and well-manicured greens that proved to be both fast and challenging. Most of the holes involve quite sloping fairways which made for numerous second shots from less than level lies, but the fairways were fairly forgiving so even high handicappers have the opportunity to keep the ball in play and achieve a decent score—that is, if your short game and putting are on that day.

In addition to a professionally groomed course that plays well, Deer Run has other amenities. All of the carts have a cleverly mounted book with individual pages for each hole showing the layout, hazards and distances. In addition, most carts are equipped with a GPS device showing distance from the cart to the green. This was certainly easier and faster than having to search for a sprinkler head to determine your yardage. There are good practice facilities with a driving range, two putting greens, and fairway and greenside bunkers. The clubhouse, which is a converted 100+ year old farmhouse, has a small pro shop and a nice pub/restaurant at which we had an excellent lunch.

Although Deer Run Golf Club may be a bit of a drive from some areas of the Twin Cities, we would highly recommend giving this beautifully kept course a try. It will provide a challenging, but satisfying, round for golfers of all levels.

SOUTHWEST

DWAN

3301 West 110th Street
Bloomington, MN 55431
Clubhouse: 952-563-8702
Golf Shop: 952-563-8702
Type: Public   Par: 68

www.ci.bloomington.mn.us

Tees	Men's	Women's	Yards
Red		65.4/110	4518
White	64.9/113	69.6/119	5275
Blue	65.8/115	70.8/121	5485

Region: Twin Cities

Course Rating

HOSPITALITY	8.36
PLAYABILITY	7.34
USABILITY	6.93
FACILITY	7.27
VALUE	5.07

OVERALL SCORE
727

Greens Fee: $28.00 (weekend)
1/2 Cart Fee: $16.00 (weekend)

Established in 1970, Dwan Golf Course is a municipal course located in a quiet residential neighborhood in south Bloomington. Dwan has an abundance of mature trees that line the fairways and dot the course so one is seldom aware of the homes that surround it. The trees are interspersed with wildflower plantings, raised flower beds, a few ponds and a number of well-placed bunkers. The course is very attractive visually and everything was beautifully maintained.

While Dwan's relatively short length (5485 yards from the tips) and six par-3 holes may make it look easy on the scorecard, it proved to be a challenge for all the golfers in our foursome. We found it provides a good challenge but not to the point of frustration. The fairways are not overly wide; however, most errant drives remain in play although not always with a clear shot to the green. They are also quite rolling which means a number of second shots will be from a less than level lie. The rough is very manageable and allows for plenty of opportunity to advance the ball. The greens are firm and fast and, as we discovered, not always easy to read.

The clubhouse is adequate but nothing to write home about. You can purchase balls and tees but that seems to be the extent of the pro shop. There is a snack bar with the usual items for both breakfast and lunch. The staff members we came in contact with were friendly and helpful including the marshal who let us know in the nicest way on the 10th tee that we were about 5 minutes behind the pace and could we pick it up a little. There is no driving range and the area to practice chipping is some distance from the clubhouse. On the day we played, this area was much in need of some mowing and attention to the practice green there. The putting green near the clubhouse was in beautiful shape and gave one a good feel for the actual greens on the course.

This course is fun for the hacker, very walkable and also has enough challenge for the lower handicap golfer. Fees are reasonable, particularly if you walk since the cart fee seems a bit high.

FOX HOLLOW

4780 Palmgren Lane NE
St. Michael, MN 55376
Clubhouse: 763-428-4468
Golf Shop: 763-428-4468
Type: Semi-Private   Par: 36/36/36

www.foxhollowgolf.net

Tees	Men's	Women's	Yards
Red		73.7/127	5797
White	70.7/128	76.6/133	6318
Blue	71.9/130		6560

Region: Twin Cities

Course Rating

HOSPITALITY	7.42
PLAYABILITY	7.26
USABILITY	8.15
FACILITY	6.69
VALUE	5.93

OVERALL SCORE
726

Greens Fee: $42.00 (weekend)
1/2 Cart Fee: $15.00 (weekend)

Located about a mile off Interstate 94 in St. Michael, Minnesota, Fox Hollow is a collection of 27 holes that provide a string of challenges for the consummate hacker.

They have an original 18 and a new "Black /Gold 9" on the other side of County Road 36 that apparently can be played in both directions.

The original 18 is a challenging collection of holes which starts deceptively easy and gets tougher. The third hole, par 3, is 156 yards over the Crow River, which isn't too tough—if you can tell yourself the river isn't there. On the back nine is an even shorter par 3 at 131 yards that is down a wicked hill and blind from the tee box. You need to hit a club you believe in. The par 5s are laid out pretty simple and provide a good chance to score well.

As far as conditions go, the tee boxes were soft and the greens rolled true but the fairways needed some serious help. Several of the fairways were covered in ant hills—picture an 8 year old with chicken pox. We asked the ranger about it and got the cordial reply, "I don't know—must be that time of season." We didn't know there was an "ant hills pop up all over the fairway" time of season. We hope they get it fixed because it really ruined a few fairways.

And that brings us to service. The life of a ranger, on the course that is, can't be too tough. He is likely retired, gets to ride around on a golf cart all day and meet what you have to believe are generally nice people. A good ranger can do a lot for a golfer's experience. Well, the aforementioned ranger had to be the most unfriendly and disgruntled man we have ever met on a course. He barely said hello and wandered around the edge of a creek for a while in a world of his own. Service in the pro shop and clubhouse was fine but not exceptional.

Fox Hollow is a nice course that can be a great course if they can eliminate the ant hills and put a big permanent smile on that ranger's face!

SOUTHWEST

FRANCIS A. GROSS

2201 St. Anthony Boulevard
Minneapolis, MN 55418
Clubhouse: 612-789-2542
Golf Shop: 612-789-2542
Type: Public   Par: 71
www.minneapolisparks.org

Tees	Men's	Women's	Yards
Forward		67.6/112	4939
Gold	63.5/107	68.0/113	5022
Standard	69.6/118	74.9/128	6348
Long	71.0/120		6631

Region: Twin Cities

Course Rating

HOSPITALITY   7.66
PLAYABILITY   6.31
USABILITY   7.71
FACILITY   5.73
VALUE   6.69

OVERALL SCORE
688

Greens Fee: $32.00 (weekend)
1/2 Cart Fee: $14.00 (weekend)

In the heart of northeast Minneapolis, Francis A. Gross Golf Course, also known as Gross National Golf Club, has been a fixture since 1925. Conveniently located just off of Interstate 35W, it is easy to get to and easy to play.

Like many urban courses, it is landlocked and what it lacks in length needs to be made up by adding traps, water and trees. The scorecard claims a longer standard course length, but since many holes didn't even have the long tees marked, it really plays from 6348 yards. Yet, for an average golfer, this length is perfect with a couple of 500+ yard par 5s and a couple of 180+ yard par 3s. Just enough length to goad you into trying to hit your irons too far.

As to interest, Gross really doesn't do as great a job. Yes, the course has mature trees and some sand bunkers and almost every hole provides the golfer a safe landing area. The course also limits the number of "lost ball" hazards like unruly rough and open water, but there is a sense of sameness to the layout with a lot of the par 4s with similar lengths and design.

A strength of this course is that it understands what hackers need on-course: bathrooms, benches and frequent visits from the food cart. Each hole had a ball washer and a bench, even for the ladies' tees, and about every third hole, a bathroom. Even more amazing, the cart person was there every third hole like clockwork. Inside the clubhouse, they have the standard food offerings, but you can order sandwiches to go and they are ready in short order.

Francis A. Gross reflects its working class roots so don't expect fancy trappings on or off the course. You'll probably notice that the course needs a bit of tending and if it is dry, your ball will roll for miles. Yet, what they save on maintenance is reflected in the prices. Gross is one of the best overall values in the Twin Cities and even the food is at working class prices with a hot dog only $2.50 and made-to-order sandwiches for only $3.75.

74

HERITAGE LINKS

8075 Lucerne Boulevard
Lakeville, MN 55044
Clubhouse: 952-440-4656
Golf Shop: 952-440-4656
Type: Public   Par: 71

www.heritagelinks.com

Tees	Men's	Women's	Yards
White		71.3/117	5145
Blue	69.7/122	75.7/126	5929
Gold	71.4/126		6320
Black	73.0/130		6672

Region: Twin Cities

Course Rating

HOSPITALITY   7.79
PLAYABILITY   7.23
USABILITY   7.11
FACILITY   6.80
VALUE   6.86

OVERALL SCORE
724

Greens Fee: $34.60 (weekend)
1/2 Cart Fee: $15.00 (weekend)

Heritage Links Golf Club in Lakeville, Minnesota, is set amongst the low rolling hills of the South Metro's farm country. The first thing you notice when walking up to the clubhouse is the well-designed practice area with putting green and driving range. The large driving range has visible yardage markers and is well maintained to give each golfer a proper practice area.

Inside the upper level of the clubhouse is the pro shop and course dining area. The pro shop has a large selection of golf equipment and apparel with the smaller items such as golf balls, tees, and gloves seemingly fair priced. They have a large selection of golf bags and clubs that are higher priced. The clubhouse has standard food options to grab a quick meal or drink during your round. Check-in for tee times was quick, easy and relatively painless thanks to the reasonably priced greens fees.

The course is a links style layout that plays deceptively longer than its 6672 yards from the back tees. The front nine holes are more wide open and playable with very few trees and limited hazards. The back nine will test your skills and patience with tighter fairways, more water hazards and well-protected greens. Heritage Links signature hole is #13, a short 270-yard par 4 with a heavily wooded tee box that leads to a large open area around the green. It is too difficult to pass up and it will tempt even the most disciplined hacker into taking the driver out of the bag. If it is your first time playing the course it is sometimes difficult to determine your distances remaining to the flag because of limited yardage markers. Every fairway has a 150-yard from the pin pole but other than that you are left judging the distance with your eyes frequently.

Heritage Links Golf Club is a fairly priced and challenging course that any hacker would be happy to have in their neighborhood. It is also perfectly suited for the average golfer to shag a bucket of balls at the driving range after work or take advantage of the inexpensive twilight pricing starting after 2 p.m.

SOUTHWEST

HIAWATHA

4553 Longfellow Avenue South
Minneapolis, MN 55407
Clubhouse: 612-724-7715
Golf Shop: 612-724-7715
Type: Public   Par: 73

www.minneapolisparks.org

V

Course Rating

HOSPITALITY	7.23
PLAYABILITY	6.65
USABILITY	8.00
FACILITY	7.61
VALUE	7.89

OVERALL SCORE
733

Greens Fee: $32.00 (weekend)
1/2 Cart Fee: $16.00 (weekend)

Tees	Men's	Women's	Yards
Red		69.3/118	5122
Gold	67.1/118	72.4/125	5685
White	69.5/123	75.3/131	6211
Blue	71.4/126		6613

Located one block east of Cedar between Interstate 94 and Crosstown 62, Hiawatha Golf Course in Minneapolis, Minnesota, is an easy course to find and a pleasure to play. The topography is gently rolling and well suited to the player that enjoys walking.

The clubhouse offers the traditional grill and has a limited supply of clothing and golf accessories. Restrooms are clean and well maintained as are the golf carts. There are no restrooms on the course but the clubhouse is centrally located and golfers pass it by every 4 holes. The beverage cart is nonexistent after Labor Day.

The golf fees are competitive and there are good deals for seniors at $26 for 18 holes and a cart. There are junior rates, twilight rates and evening rates as well as patron cards. Lessons are available as are junior golf camps.

This course is very well maintained with lush, green fairways, tees and greens. It does, however, offer a challenge to the average hacker. The fairways are narrow and well guarded by trees. Venturing off to the right or left will leave the hacker a difficult shot through the trees or a punch-out back to the fairway. The greens are postage stamp in size but they are not too difficult.

Overall, hackers will have their share of frustration but the course is well worth your time and it is difficult to lose balls as the course rough is cut short and the grass under the trees is well mowed. The competitive rates and the gently rolling and wooded course make this city course a must even though you may find it a bit difficult for the 20+ handicapper.

Alexandria, Minnesota, native and PGA Professional Tom Lehman, winner of the 1996 British Open and 1996 PGA Player of the Year, has his brother, Jim Lehman, Jr., as his agent.

SOUTHWEST

HYLAND GREENS Exec. 18

10100 Normandale Boulevard
Bloomington, MN 55437
Clubhouse: 952-563-8868
Golf Shop: 952-563-8868
Type: Public   Par: 54
www.ci.bloomington.mn.us

Tees	Men's	Women's	Yards
Standard	54.0	54.0	2820

Course Rating

HOSPITALITY	8.69
PLAYABILITY	6.00
USABILITY	7.26
FACILITY	6.25
VALUE	5.98

OVERALL SCORE
696

Greens Fee: $23.00 (weekend)
1/2 Cart Fee: $10.00 (weekend)

In less than three hours you should be able to play Hyland Greens Golf Course, a compact executive eighteen. Located in Bloomington, Minnesota, the course is actually two separate 9-hole courses with very fancy names: the long-9 and the short-9. As with any par-3 course, you can leave your driver in the car because the longest hole is just 193 yards.

As you enter the parking lot, you've got a small clubhouse in front of you and the driving range to your right. The range has separate hitting bays, but you'll tee off on permanent mats because there is no option for hitting off the grass. The clubhouse is very simple and you can tell by the few golf carts that this course is very popular with walkers. A small putting green is available just behind the clubhouse and inside the building is just the basics in both the food and sitting area.

The first tee for both courses is just steps from the clubhouse's front door so you can wait for your tee time sipping a beer inside. Interestingly, the long-9 takes reservations and the short-9 doesn't. Also, you can't play all eighteen together. You pay for one course ($13 for the long course), check back in and then pay for the second ($10 for the short course).

The course itself is nicely manicured, if a bit austere. There is very little by way of hazards, except a few holes where you will have to hit around or over water hazards. The holes are pretty straightforward with typical lengths of 135, 174 and 193 yards on the long course and holes as short as 90 yards on the short course. Water is available on the course and there is at least one bathroom for each course. Food in the clubhouse is basic course grub and is quite reasonably priced.

If pace of play is what you are looking for you'll be able to complete the long-9 in 1 ½ hours and the short-9 even faster. If this course ever becomes a 4-hour ordeal then you are wasting way too much time. Leave your woods at home and make this a course where you work on your irons. Once you have solved them at this course, you'll be well on your way to having success with them at a longer course.

SOUTHWEST

LAKEVIEW

405 North Arm Drive
Mound, MN 55364
Clubhouse: 952-472-3459
Golf Shop: 952-472-3459
Type: Public   Par: 69

www.lakeviewgolfoforono.com

Tees	Men's	Women's	Yards
Red		68.6/113	4907
White	65.9/111	70.9/118	5322
Blue	66.8/112		5517

Region: Twin Cities

Course Rating

HOSPITALITY   7.85
PLAYABILITY   6.69
USABILITY   7.78
FACILITY   6.99
VALUE   `   5.56

OVERALL SCORE
713

Greens Fee: $29.00 (weekend)
1/2 Cart Fee: $14.00 (weekend)

Before Pioneer Creek, Timber Creek, Bluff Creek, Deer Run and Chaska Town Course, there was Lakeview Golf Course in Orono, Minnesota. Built in 1952, it is one of the oldest courses on the west side of the Twin Cities and was built before the age of titanium, graphite and space-age golf balls.

The course has no driving range, has a very small practice green and parking area, a cramped waiting area to tee off and a simple clubhouse. It was built before golf carts were common and before the Twin Cities grew out to meet the course. It doesn't have much by way of the 19th hole except a charming little patio with a few tables. Yet, you don't visit Lakeview for the clubhouse, you come for the car trip around Lake Minnetonka, charming horse farms, and most certainly the golf.

Lakeview is a compact course at 5517 yards, and has many mature trees and a beautiful pond that makes for a wonderful approach shot on the par-4 #13. Don't let the course's lack of length fool you. It isn't as easy as it sounds. The course does all it can to make life difficult with contoured greens and blind approach shots. Although you only really need to pull out your driver on three holes, it will punish you if you land your ball in the wrong place. Overall, it is a very walkable course with a smart layout and short distances between green and tee box.

The course is well maintained and it looks like it puts most of its money there because on-course amenities are few with only one bathroom witnessed when we were there and no water coolers, so bring your own. A typical round can be completed in 3 ½ hours, but one thing to be aware of is if you plan on playing during a busy summer weekend, expect it to back up.

This course is one of those that doesn't get the attention it deserves and has quietly stood the test of time for more than 55 years. When you decide to play Lakeview, you are also getting a great value at only $29 for a weekend round, well worth the price of admission and one of the best deals in the Twin Cities.

SOUTHWEST

LEGENDS

8670 Credit River Boulevard
Prior Lake, MN 55372
Clubhouse: 952-226-4777
Golf Shop: 952-226-4777
Type: Public   Par: 72
www.legendsgc.com

Region: Twin Cities

Course Rating

F

HOSPITALITY	8.68
PLAYABILITY	8.05
USABILITY	8.36
FACILITY	8.69
VALUE	5.68

OVERALL SCORE
813

Tees	Men's	Women's	Yards
Gold		71.3/127	5297
White	69.6/133	75.5/136	6046
Blue	71.3/136		6418
Black	72.6/139		6702
Silver	74.2/142		7058

Greens Fee: $79.00 (weekend)
1/2 Cart Fee: $15.00 (weekend)

Prior Lake, Minnesota, is at the center of some of the best golf courses in the Twin Cities. With The Wilds, The Meadows at Mystic Lake and Legends all located in the city, there should be no complaints from area golfers.

Legends, perhaps a bit lesser known than the others, is a formidable competitor. It is a country club experience at a reasonable price point. The grounds are nicely laid out with a large parking lot, a club drop-off site, putting and pitching areas, a nicely appointed clubhouse with an excellent bar/restaurant area that is a must for the 19th hole and an expansive outdoor grill/patio. The course itself was in excellent condition, even later in the season. The signage is very good and the cart paths are paved and always nearby. Each cart has GPS and for a course as challenging as Legends, a godsend for certain shots.

Approaching the first tee doesn't begin to tell you the experience you will have. In fact, the front nine is considered easier to play than the back, but that is only because the fairways might be a bit wider. What awaits the unsuspecting golfer is a course that will challenge you with shots over water, across scrub areas, blind approaches, sand trap city and big doglegs. The course has it all and it isn't for the faint of heart.

This is not a course that a hacker should play if he/she expects to shoot low. It isn't going to happen. You might think you've solved the course on one hole by making a par, but it is only a temporary condition and it will bite you back. The course has been designed to require every club in your bag and smart course management. Just to make things worse, it will force you to hit terrifying shots over water requiring carries of at least 150 yards. If you are aquaphobic, you'll be sorry.

This is a course that you should treat yourself to at least once a season because it is worth the extra cost. It might not be the place you have your best round, but it will be a highlight of your summer and give you a sense of how the other half lives.

SOUTHWEST

MEADOWBROOK

201 Meadowbrook Road
Hopkins, MN 55343
Clubhouse: 952-929-2077
Golf Shop: 952-929-2077
Type: Public   Par: 72

www.minneapolisparks.org

Tees	Men's	Women's	Yards
Red		69.5/121	4934
Yellow	68.2/124	73.4/129	5640
White	71.0/130		6252
Blue	72.3/132		6529

Region: Twin Cities

Course Rating

HOSPITALITY	7.65
PLAYABILITY	6.18
USABILITY	6.82
FACILITY	5.77
VALUE	5.26

OVERALL SCORE
652

Greens Fee: $32.00 (weekend)
1/2 Cart Fee: $14.00 (weekend)

Located right off Excelsior Boulevard in Hopkins, Minnesota, Meadowbrook is run and operated by the Minneapolis Parks and Recreation Board. As part of the park system, it is a course built very much to the same dynamics as Theodore Wirth, Columbia, or Hiawatha. These park courses are designed towards the playing abilities of the average golfer and are meant to cater towards the needs of that type of player. Meadowbrook slides perfectly into this category.

There is no fancy clubhouse or any "collared shirts only" signs waiting for you at Meadowbrook, and it has a very down-to-earth feel about it right away. It does lack a driving range to get warmed up, but the course will be very manageable when you get going.

Starting out with two par 5s in the first four holes means you want to get your swing going early because the 5th, 3rd, and 1st handicapped holes are coming up next. The back nine plays just a tad longer, but most of the yardage comes on the par 4s and par 5s, as the two par 3s on the back play a very modest 126 and 135 yards. We've never been big fans of wedge par 3s, it gives a rinky-dink feel to a course, but if you're struggling on the back side, the two par 3s offer a nice break.

For the most part, Meadowbrook is very straightforward. There's trouble to be found, but you have to go well out of your way to look for it most of the time, and even if you do find it there's usually a manageable way to get around it. If you're going to throw up a big number here, it's not going to be because the course is asking you to make a shot you're not capable of making. As part of the park system, the greens fees are very affordable and at $32 on the weekend, the price is tough to beat. Overall, Meadowbrook is a good dollar-for-dollar value, especially for twilight rates.

The couch-surrounded big screen TV in the clubhouse showing the Packers losing when we walked in didn't hurt either.

PIONEER CREEK

705 Copeland Road
Maple Plain, MN 55359
Clubhouse: 952-955-3982
Golf Shop: 952-955-3982
Type: Public   Par: 72

www.pioneercreek.com

Tees	Men's	Women's	Yards
Red		69.7/121	5147
Gold	68.4/123	73.5/129	5840
White	70.4/128	76.0/134	6291
Blue	72.0/130		6618
Black	73.5/133		6953

Region: Twin Cities

Course Rating

HOSPITALITY	6.97
PLAYABILITY	5.66
USABILITY	6.07
FACILITY	5.75
VALUE	4.80

OVERALL SCORE
600

Greens Fee: $39.00 (weekend)
1/2 Cart Fee: $14.00 (weekend)

If you are looking for golf on the west side of the Twin Cities, Pioneer Creek Golf Course in Maple Plain, Minnesota, can be approached on County Road 6 from either direction and you will see the clubhouse on the north side of the road. At the time of this writing we found the area a little dusty as there was new construction going on across the road from the clubhouse so roll up your windows.

This is a typical farm-country golf course with a nice layout. The tee boxes, rough and greens were in good shape but the fairways were hard and dry. There is a nice mixture of hazards (woods, water, sand and swamp) but only two holes really challenge accuracy. The greens are relatively small and the cups all seem to be elevated, making putts a challenge. There is little in the way of signage but the asphalt cart paths take the golfer from one hole to the next without the need for signs. There is not a level fairway on the course and the golf course's rolling contours makes for a good workout for the walker.

The course has many on-course porta-potties so a pit stop is just a few holes away. One sour note was the cleanliness and condition of the golf carts. Most carts could use a cleaning and the one we drove emitted a piercing whine from the rear axle that gave us a headache by the end of the round.

The log cabin clubhouse is pretty bare bones but was clean and the staff cordial and helpful. It offers the traditional golf course grub (snack bar) and a decent collection of gear and clothing. No great deals but some nice looking stuff. Fees for golf, driving range and carts are typical of this type of country course so you should be able to find a rate that will fit your budget.

There are enough challenges to make the course interesting but the wide fairways should keep you out of trouble most of the time with an opportunity for par on most holes and a birdie shot every now and then. For a little refreshment after the game, try the Ox Yoke Inn in Lyndale just a couple blocks east of Copeland on 92 heading towards St. Boni.

SOUTHWEST

RIDGES AT SAND CREEK

Region: Twin Cities

21775 Ridges Drive
Jordan, MN 55352
Clubhouse: 952-492-2644
Golf Shop: 952-492-2644
Type: Public   Par: 72

www.ridgesatsandcreek.com

H

Course Rating

HOSPITALITY	9.52
PLAYABILITY	8.02
USABILITY	6.98
FACILITY	7.98
VALUE	6.98

OVERALL SCORE
808

Greens Fee: $43.00 (weekend)
1/2 Cart Fee: $15.00 (weekend)

Tees	Men's	Women's	Yards
Red		70.2/123	5136
Gold	68.1/126	73.5/131	5739
White	69.8/130	75.6/135	6115
Blue	71.8/134		6547
Black	73.6/137		6936

Ridges at Sand Creek is a beautiful course in Jordan, Minnesota, that combines everything a hacker needs to be successful—short rough, short par 3s and a detailed scorecard outlining each hole.

Located just off Highway 21, the Ridges clubhouse is two stories and combines a pro shop, banquet center and restaurant offering a full menu (our post-round quesadillas were better than we've had at several chain restaurants). The staff are warm and welcoming and ready to assist and seem to do it all with a smile. Mike Malone, the owner, is especially nice and willing to "talk golf" with the visitors.

A large practice green gives golfers a chance to get a feel for the greens without feeling crowded. The nearby driving range is not very impressive but suffices for getting a few swings in before stepping to the first tee.

The course feels like it is really two courses in one. About six of the holes are wide open where an errant drive won't hurt you very much. But the remaining twelve are cut out of the forest like a hot ice cream scoop through a pint of Rocky Road. Trees line the fairways and make a towering backdrop behind the greens. Creeks run across the fairways in conspicuous places but they were incredibly dry for the midsummer. The par 3s on the course are quite short, including an incredibly dainty 90-yarder on the back nine. The rough is not long so a pushed or pulled drive, while not ideal, won't kill you.

The biggest complaint would have to be the condition of some of the tee boxes. A rubber mallet was literally needed to pound a tee into the box and that tee was then snapped like a twig upon impact with the driver. A little more water would seem to be the obvious cure. The greens had a good pace to them and pin placement was generally favorable to the golfer. Finding Ridges is quite easy with just one exit off of Highway 169 putting you right at the course. Make sure to bring a few extra balls for those tree-lined holes.

STONEBROOKE

2693 County Road 79
Shakopee, MN 55379
Clubhouse: 952-496-3171
Golf Shop: 952-496-3171
Type: Public   Par: 71

www.stonebrooke.com

Tees	Men's	Women's	Yards
Red		69.4/124	4830
White	68.5/131	74.4/134	5728
Blue	70.2/135	76.5/139	6104
Black	71.9/138		6475

Course Rating

HOSPITALITY	8.70
PLAYABILITY	7.36
USABILITY	8.87
FACILITY	8.68
VALUE	6.20

U
F

OVERALL SCORE
808

Greens Fee: $55.50 (weekend)
1/2 Cart Fee: $16.00 (weekend)

Stonebrooke Golf Club, located in Shakopee, Minnesota, was developed in 1989 by Laurent Companies which builds homes and master-planned communities. Stonebrooke reflects this in the clubhouse design, the wonderful landscaping and maintenance of the course.

The driving range is located across the road near the Waters Edge executive course, which is also part of the Stonebrooke golf complex. This requires taking a golf cart to get to the range. The practice putting green is on a slope and we couldn't find any area on the putting green where there was a flat, straight putt. The course plays to a par 71.

The course has gently rolling fairways with generous fairway widths, trees, a number of environmentally sensitive areas, swamps, small ponds and little streams. Some of the bridges over the creek are miniature covered bridges. For the men there are four forced carries over water or swamps, of about 165–185 yards from the white tees. The greens provide a formidable challenge as they are quite large, faster than the average and have many undulations.

The signature hole is #8. The hole is only 320 yards, but from the white tee you need a drive to carry from 165–185 yards across the bay of the lake. Once teeing off you will load your clubs and cart on a pontoon boat which will ferry you across the bay to the fairway. All the cart paths are blacktopped and it's easy to navigate the course. There is good signage throughout. The gas-powered carts all have GPS.

Stonebrooke has a wide variety of rates. If you book your tee time online you will receive a free golf cart. They have a wonderful website which has a variety of information and some neat course pictures, too.

Stonebrooke is a well-maintained, well-run golf course that is a good test of golf and strives to provide a country club experience at a cost between an average and an upscale golf course.

SOUTHWEST

83

THE MEADOWS

2400 Mystic Lake Drive
Prior Lake, MN 55372
Clubhouse: 952-233-5533
Golf Shop: 952-233-5533
Type: Public   Par: 72

www.mysticlakegolf.com

Tees	Men's	Women's	Yards
Gold		71.2/131	5293
Green	68.5/134	74.1/137	5823
White	70.8/139	76.9/143	6318
Blue	72.3/142		6668
Black	74.6/146		7144

Region: Twin Cities

Course Rating

HOSPITALITY	8.20
PLAYABILITY	8.71
USABILITY	7.45
FACILITY	7.00
VALUE	5.34

OVERALL SCORE
774

Greens Fee: $85.00 (weekend)
1/2 Cart Fee: included in fee

The Meadows at Mystic Lake is located behind Mystic Lake Casino in Prior Lake, Minnesota. This is a championship course and it plays that way. This is a very nice layout with many picturesque features like waterfalls, wildlife statues, streams, lakes and some very nice architecture. We suppose that all those features are there to take your mind off the fact that for some reason, you can't figure out why you can't get a par to save your life. This is not a very hacker-friendly course. If you know the layout and play some good course management, you might be able to get in the low 90s, but it's unlikely.

Most fairways are set in a semivalley with raised borders framing the hole. Those borders are filled with high, dense, native prairie grasses, which makes finding your ball nearly impossible and playing from there downright wicked.

In general, throughout the regular playing season, this course is in top condition with tee boxes, fairways and greens in great shape. It better be for the price they are asking. However, this review was done near the end of October and although they had a reduced rate, the conditions were quite poor.

Tee boxes were in need of repair due to divots and a couple were not even flat and level. Fairways were a mixed bag with some being fine and in good condition and others punched and sanded. Greens were okay except there seemed to be an inconsistency in speed and amount of break from one green to another. Carts were nice, newer electric models with GPS.

At the turn, there is grill service and a patio area where we were greeted by a very nice and polite server willing to help except he had almost no items available from the menu at 12:30 p.m. The 19th hole is a nice restaurant with good reasonably priced food, but remember this facility is dry and does not serve alcohol.

Final thought. This is a challenging picturesque course that you play once, maybe twice a year. Just think that you are on vacation at a resort course and are there to enjoy yourself and not worry about what will be your final score.

THE WILDS

3151 Wilds Ridge
Prior Lake, MN 55372
Clubhouse: 952-445-3500
Golf Shop: 952-445-3500 x4
Type: Public   Par: 72

www.golfthewilds.com

Tees	Men's	Women's	Yards
Forward	65.9/134	71.1/132	5118
Wilds	71.0/145	77.3/145	6241
Champion	72.1/147		6489
Weiskopf	74.5/152		7025

Course Rating

HOSPITALITY	8.90
PLAYABILITY	8.08
USABILITY	8.22
FACILITY	7.51
VALUE	6.32

OVERALL SCORE
805

Greens Fee: $80.00 (weekend)
1/2 Cart Fee: $16.00 (weekend)

If you think that The Wilds in Prior Lake, Minnesota, considered the Twin Cities first upscale public course when it opened in 1996, is too rich for your blood, think again. Times have changed and with a patronage card, you can snag tee time as low as $55 a round (includes cart and free range balls). It may surprise you how golfing luxury can fit into your budget.

The Tom Weiskopf-designed course has everything you'd expect from a quality track: imaginative course layout, well-kept fairways and challenging greens. With tee boxes from 5118 to 7025 yards, it is able to accommodate players of various skill levels. This reviewer played with a three-handicapper and the course challenged us all. The key to success here is keeping your ego in check and choosing the right tee box for your game.

If you are a straight ball hitter you should have nothing to worry about here. If you are not, don't think of the long carries you will be required to hit or the deep rough if your shot goes off line. Also don't think of the 152 slope or the 74.5 par rating from the Weiskopf tees either. Those things will play with your head.

Like any quality course, The Wilds clubhouse is right out of a country club. Well appointed, there is a large pro shop, a reasonably priced restaurant and banquet facilities that can accommodate 350 people. Staying for the 19th hole is an easy decision in the great bar with a friendly barkeep.

Very popular for corporate events (they do over 110 events annually), the course gets a lot of use and can be busy. The course is a bit thin on distance markers and you'll see a lot of rooftops in the fully developed neighborhood surrounding the course, but try to remember to ask at the pro shop for the purple yardage book that will tell you everything you need to know about playing the course.

If you want to treat yourself to a country club experience on a hacker's budget, The Wilds is one of the top courses in the South Metro, especially towards the end of the season when you can take advantage of their "pay the temperature" special.

SOUTHWEST

85

THEODORE WIRTH

1301 Theodore Wirth Parkway
Minneapolis, MN 55422
Clubhouse: 763-522-4584
Golf Shop: 763-522-4584
Type: Public   Par: 72

www.minneapolisparks.org

Tees	Men's	Women's	Yards
Red		71.2/117	5285
Gold	68.1/124	73.4/121	5666
White	70.9/130	76.9/128	6295
Blue	72.2/132		6575

Region: Twin Cities

Course Rating

HOSPITALITY   7.72
PLAYABILITY   6.59
USABILITY   7.58
FACILITY   6.27
VALUE   6.78

OVERALL SCORE
704

Greens Fee: $30.00 (weekend)
1/2 Cart Fee: $14.00 (weekend)

If you are a short straight hitter, this is the course you can win on! But if you like to hit the 250–300 yard bombs that don't always go straight, don't bet the farm when you are playing Theodore Wirth Golf Course in Golden Valley, Minnesota. For a Minneapolis Park's run golf course, Theodore Wirth will give you a challenge at a reasonable price. Located just off of Highway 55, it is easy to get to. Also the area has a lot to offer the rest of the non-golfers while you enjoy this 18-hole course that was established in 1916.

The Minneapolis Parks board does its best to keep the tees, fairways, greens, and first cut of rough in good playing condition. For the extras, cart paths, sand traps, course ranger, food service, the park could use some more funding to improve these services. The 18-hole par 72 course plays 6295 yards from the white tees—which is not long, but you better hit it straight! The fairways are well groomed, and in the rough you can usually find your ball. But leave the clubs that you slice with in the bag. Past the first cut of rough are heavy woods or water areas. Also, there are a number of tee-offs where you are faced with blind shots.

The layout of the front nine holes is very friendly for the walker. The back nine holes will challenge that same walker's stamina. Every hole on the back, except the par-5 #12, has an incline and/or decline that you have to contend with. Each hole has the 100, 150, and 200 yardage markers, along with some sprinkler head markers. Tee-off signage is adequate. The first hole is the only one to provide extra information on distance to the water. Benches, garbage cans and ball washers are at each tee-off, and there is a beverage cart. Porta-potties are conveniently located on the course but only one rain shelter was observed. Overall the whole course setting with mature trees, natural water hazards and the occassional deer running through at dusk cannot be beat.

After our first experience with Theodore Wirth Golf Course would we play it again? Yes, and we would leave our driver in the bag!

TIMBER CREEK

9750 County Road 24
Watertown, MN 55388
Clubhouse: 952-955-3600
Golf Shop: 952-955-3600
Type: Semi-Private   Par: 72

www.timbercreekgolf.com

Tees	Men's	Women's	Yards
Red		71.8/129	5331
Gold	67.4/126	72.4/131	5436
White	70.6/133	76.3/139	6137
Blue	71.7/136	77.7/142	6390
Black	72.8/137		6621

Region: Twin Cities

Course Rating

HOSPITALITY	7.71
PLAYABILITY	7.20
USABILITY	6.49
FACILITY	6.72
VALUE	6.44

OVERALL SCORE
704

Greens Fee: $34.00 (weekend)
1/2 Cart Fee: $14.00 (weekend)

On the west side of the Twin Cities is a gem of a course. Nestled next to horse and hobby farms, Timber Creek is a quiet example of rural golf. With tight tree-lined fairways and a few intimidating gimmick holes, the course is 6621 yards from the tips and without local knowledge, it plays a lot longer than advertised.

When checking in, the guy at the front desk asked if we wanted a tip sheet so we'd have a better idea of how to play the course (they called it their virtual caddy). We declined. Big mistake. This is not a wide-open urban track where you can spray your ball in all directions. Course management, always hard for a hacker, is a very good idea.

Approaching the course from the highway you might miss Timber Creek's unassuming signage (if you see horses, you've gone too far). Once there, the rut-filled gravel entrance road might make you think this is a neglected and undermaintained course. Not so. The course was lush, tree-lined and in great shape. The only knock on maintenance was that the greens had a lot of small dead spots and a few tee boxes were completely denuded of turf which seemed very out-of-character to the rest of the course.

The staff was quite friendly in a small town sort of way. Upon arriving, you felt that this was your local golf club and you had been playing here for years. The clubhouse is casual, the food reasonable but unremarkable, and the facility layout compact. One unusual course rule was that you can't drive the golf carts onto the parking lot so try to park close to the clubhouse when you arrive.

The pricing does have a bias toward locals, but there are also a lot of off-time and senior specials available. Timber Creek is the kind of course you must play more than once before you see it reflected in your score. It is not really a good walking course and you have numerous opportunities to find yourself in trouble spots (the reviewer hit six trees incidentally), but it will surely grow on you the more you play it. If you live on the west side of the Twin Cities and haven't ever played this course, it's worth the extra few miles for a visit.

SOUTHWEST

87

VALLEY VIEW

23795 Laredo Avenue
Belle Plaine, MN 56011
Clubhouse: 952-873-4653
Golf Shop: 952-873-4653
Type: Public   Par: 71

www.vvgolf.com

Tees	Men's	Women's	Yards
Red		69.8/120	4921
Gold	68.5/123	74.0/128	5667
White	69.9/125	75.6/132	5962
Blue	71.0/128		6208

Region: Twin Cities

Course Rating

HOSPITALITY	6.59
PLAYABILITY	6.58
USABILITY	7.20
FACILITY	5.78
VALUE	6.31

OVERALL SCORE
656

Greens Fee: $35.00 (weekend)
1/2 Cart Fee: $16.00 (weekend)

Located in Belle Plaine, Minnesota, Valley View Golf Course is reasonably priced and moderately challenging but it feels cramped as though they squeezed 18 holes of golf into an area with enough acres for 16 holes. Combine that with some ugly customer service and the course left us with a lot to be desired.

Valley View was very easy to find and the clubhouse had a very welcoming appeal as we checked in for our round. The woman in the pro shop checked us in, gave us cart keys and pointed us in the direction of the carts. Things were off to a great start. They started to slide as we got outside. Our cart was drenched in dew and we ended up having to use our golf towel to wipe down the whole cart.

The practice area includes a nice putting green, a chipping area and a driving range. While not immaculate (the putting green was incredibly sandy), they do the trick to help iron out the kinks before the first tee.

The course starts with a relatively easy hole, par-4 dogleg right. Just don't slice it or you'll be hunting amongst range balls to find it and hitting three as it is out-of-bounds. The holes continued to be moderately challenging with shots over water and around trees which was fun but every hole seemed cramped.

After our initial encounter in the pro shop, the service was paltry the rest of the way. The call box on #8 for food didn't work after three attempts to call for a hot dog. The cart girl we stopped on #9 (a ridiculously long 230-yard par 3) had no input on it and said "I just drive the cart." No brats were ready in the clubhouse and the kid behind the counter swore the intercom system worked. All he could offer was the "hot dogs I just put out in the crock pot over there." We already felt like we were risking our lives on some of the holes on the course; we weren't about to risk food poisoning from the clubhouse.

Overall the golf was pretty good, the service was pretty bad and the whole experience was just okay. We hope if we're ever back it leaves us with a better impression.

Twin Cities Courses

Afton Alps
Bellwood Oaks
Como
Country Air
Eagle Valley
Emerald Greens (brnz/gold)
Emerald Greens (silver/plat)
Fountain Valley
Goodrich
Hidden Greens
Highland National
Inver Wood

Keller
Les Bolstad
Mississippi Dunes
Oak Marsh
Parkview
Phalen Park
Prestwick
Rich Valley
River Oaks
Southern Hills
Valleywood

Joel Goldstrand, a golf course architect from Minneapolis, has designed more than 80 golf courses in the Upper Midwest. His first project in 1969 was in Worthington, Minnesota.

AFTON ALPS

6600 Peller Avenue South
Hastings, MN 55033
Clubhouse: 651-436-1320
Golf Shop: 651-436-1320
Type: Public   Par: 72

www.aftonalps.com

Tees	Men's	Women's	Yards
Red		68.6/117	4789
White	67.7/114	72.8/127	5556
Blue	68.9/116	74.3/130	5823

Course Rating

HOSPITALITY	8.13
PLAYABILITY	6.52
USABILITY	6.31
FACILITY	5.67
VALUE	5.43

OVERALL SCORE
664

Greens Fee: $26.00 (weekend)
1/2 Cart Fee: $12.00 (weekend)

Afton Alps Golf Course in Afton, Minnesota, is part of the year-round Afton Alps recreational area, and located adjacent to Afton State Park, but technically has a Hastings, Minnesota address. It is open to the public and a nicely distanced course at 5823 yards from the blue tees. Golf carts are available, and necessary.

There are two practice greens and one is set up for chipping. The course does not offer a driving range. In the clubhouse there is lots of seating, a grill, and they do have full bar service. There is also a limited amount of golf items for purchase. The staff was very friendly and after our round came out to meet us and ask if we wanted them to keep the grill opened for us, as they were getting ready to close, but would be happy to stay if we wanted.

Afton Alps really is two different golf courses in one. The front nine plays very nicely and is well laid out. Greens are reachable in regulation, and we found the course to be very wide open and hazards placed in the appropriate locations. We did enjoy the front nine, but found the back nine to be far different. The back nine is laid out almost entirely within the Afton Alps ski slopes, making for a very hilly and sometimes odd layout. You are literally playing golf on the same slopes that you can ski on in the winter. It really seemed to be an afterthought to have holes here, tee boxes poorly placed, blind shots around corners, ski lifts surrounding holes and snowmaking machines and piping around the course. On the plus side, there are some very scenic vantage points on the back nine, with some nice views of the St. Croix River Valley. We even spotted three deer and a raccoon on the course.

We found this course just okay. Guess it would be fair to say we felt kind of "duped." We came for 18 holes of golf and we got 9. The second nine was more of a tour of the ski resort without the snow. Would we return? Maybe, but there are many more comparable choices that would be more enjoyable. Most likely, the next time we'd return, it would be with our skis, to experience the more appropriate use of this particular parcel of real estate.

BELLWOOD OAKS

13239 210th Street East
Hastings, MN 55033
Clubhouse: 651-437-4141
Golf Shop: 651-437-4141
Type: Public   Par: 73
www.bellwoodoaksgolf.com

Tees	Men's	Women's	Yards
Red		70.0/120	5124
Gold	69.5/121	74.4/129	5916
White	72.1/126	77.6/135	6487
Blue	73.5/129		6791

Region: Twin Cities

Course Rating

HOSPITALITY	7.46
PLAYABILITY	7.28
USABILITY	8.10
FACILITY	7.57
VALUE	5.28

OVERALL SCORE
733

Greens Fee: $29.00 (weekend)
1/2 Cart Fee: $15.00 (weekend)

Bellwood Oaks Golf Club is located about five minutes south of Hastings, Minnesota, just off Highway 61. We golfed on a Monday morning and there were 10 to 12 golfers at the first tee. We were on time and had no wait at the first hole. There is a practice green and an 8-station driving range on site. Check-in is in a small building close to the first tee.

If you are hungry, or think you are going to be, better make sure you get something before you get here. There is a very limited amount of snacks and microwave sandwiches available. A few tables in the check-in building is the extent of the clubhouse amenities.

We really liked this course. It was a "no frills" experience other than the golf, but the round itself was very enjoyable. We found the course to be exceedingly well kept, and very hacker friendly. There is not an abundance of flora and fauna, but the holes are nevertheless very nice and give you a peaceful feeling. The rough was a bit on the long side, but not overly so. Greens were large, and flat for the most part; some gradual slopes here and there make them challenging on only a few holes. The greens were in excellent condition and the flags on this particular day were very fairly placed. The thing we liked most about this course was the fact that all holes were very reachable in regulation. If you drive an average distance and keep the ball in the fairway, you will have an excellent chance to reach the green and score well. If you do have the cursed slice or hook on your drives, don't worry, the course is open enough that you still have a chance to recover and score. There are 34 groomed bunkers on the course, and 3 holes have water, but all were fairly placed and the water was flagged with a striped pole to let you know it was there. Out-of-bounds markers come into play on only a few holes, and you really are out-of-bounds when you cross them.

Again, the best part of the day was the golf, just like it should be. Great course, in great condition, and very hacker friendly. This is a course we will surely visit again.

COMO

1431 North Lexington Parkway
St. Paul, MN 55103
Clubhouse: 651-488-9679
Golf Shop: 651-488-9673
Type: Public   Par: 70
www.golfstpaul.org

Region: Twin Cities

Course Rating

HOSPITALITY	6.83
PLAYABILITY	6.07
USABILITY	6.36
FACILITY	5.37
VALUE	5.88

OVERALL SCORE
619

Greens Fee: $30.00 (weekend)
1/2 Cart Fee: $14.00 (weekend)

Tees	Men's	Women's	Yards
Red		69.8/121	5077
White	67.5/122		5581
Blue	68.6/124		5842

Nestled within the extensive Como Park, St. Paul's Como Golf Course has been a fixture in the city since 1929. Initially opened as a 9-hole course, it was extensively redesigned in 1988, with new a layout, clubhouse and cart storage area.

The facility is compact, with the parking just steps from the clubhouse and the power cart corral. The clubhouse is pretty bare bones, but does have a nice grill with the standard food and drinks at the turn. The sitting areas have an excellent view of the course from the elevation of the clubhouse, but the inside seating is not meant to keep you there very long.

Although the grill service was good and attentive, the pro shop, cart tender and on-course service was a bit spotty. It might have been because we visited on a Thursday afternoon, but the facility seemed to be a bit understaffed that day.

The course tries hard to overcome its lack of length and is only partially successful. It does have three picturesque ponds, but few hazards come into play except for an imposing par-5 #8 with the green tucked behind one of those ponds. The course, like a lot of city courses, has seen a lot of use. There were a number of "under construction" areas, its fairways were a bit overdry and the greens often had brown spots on their surfaces. Signage was also very poor with directional information spray painted in white on the asphalt cart paths. Also, if there were tee box distance signs, they were well hidden. The course also lacks a driving range because there is no place to put it.

For value-priced golf, Como is quite economical at $30 for 18 holes. If you are looking for a fast round in the City of St. Paul, Como Golf Course should be considered an option but just remember, it plays more like a long executive course than it does a regulation length par 72. After your round, for better food, just walk down the hill to the Lakeside Pavilion and stop in at the Black Bear Crossings coffee shop.

SOUTHEAST

92

COUNTRY AIR Exec. 18

404 Lake Elmo Avenue North
Lake Elmo, MN 55042
Clubhouse: 651-436-7888
Golf Shop: 651-436-7888
Type: Public   Par: 54
www.countryairgolfpark.com

Tees	Men's	Women's	Yards
Red	54.0	54.0	1042

Region: Twin Cities

Course Rating
HOSPITALITY   9.01
PLAYABILITY   6.90
USABILITY   8.05
FACILITY   6.20
VALUE   7.27

OVERALL SCORE
759

Greens Fee: $15.00 (weekend)
1/2 Cart Fee: no carts available

Country Air Golf Park, located just south of Interstate 94 in Lake Elmo, Minnesota, has something for everyone. For one thing, it has a heated driving range that is open year round. Another portion of the driving range provides choices of hitting off natural grass or artificial turf, and a large practice putting green and bunker. It seems the main attraction is the 18-hole pitch and putt course.

The course is a jaunt from the clubhouse, and it's easy to think the tenth hole is really the first hole. The holes are labeled by the flags on the greens, but if there isn't a wind, it may be difficult to determine the hole number. Small signs point from one hole to the next, so it's a good idea to follow the scorecard layout. Since the holes crisscross in close proximity, one may want to be on the lookout for errant golf balls if the course is busy. The length of the holes range from 40 to 75 yards making Country Air the perfect spot to practice one's short game. In fact, the manager suggests that one needs to use only a pitching wedge and putter to play the course.

Families with young children find it an ideal spot to bring the kids who are transitioning from miniature golf to an actual 18-hole format. Adults will also enjoy the setup while working to improve their shorter shots and putting. Most of the holes have at least one sand trap, although none contain a rake. The fairways provide slight hills and twists which lead to greens that are nearly perfectly groomed. A small creek meanders through the nicely landscaped course.

Country Air offers lessons for both juniors and adults, along with leagues, tournaments, and events. The clubhouse presents few amenities except for some snacks and beverages. It's a great spot to bring younger golfers, and parents could practice their short game at the same time.

SOUTHEAST

EAGLE VALLEY

2600 Double Eagle Lane
Woodbury, MN 55129
Clubhouse: 651-714-3750
Golf Shop: 651-714-3750
Type: Public   Par: 72

www.eaglevalleygc.com

Course Rating

HOSPITALITY	9.32
PLAYABILITY	8.12
USABILITY	8.15
FACILITY	7.08
VALUE	6.66

H

OVERALL SCORE
812

Greens Fee: $40.00 (weekend)
1/2 Cart Fee: $16.00 (weekend)

Tees	Men's	Women's	Yards
Red		69.7/119	5207
White	69.7/124	75.0/130	6165
Blue	71.5/128	77.2/135	6570
Black	73.1/131		6907

Eagle Valley Golf Course, off Interstate 94 in Woodbury, is our nominee for "Retired Guy Who Has the Job I Want/Ranger of the Year" award. From a cordial welcome at the first tee, to telling stories of ridiculous golfers he's seen on the course, to a few check-ins throughout the rest of the round—every course should have employees who exhibit this type of service. He even brought a playing partner's wedge up to him from a previous hole before he had time to realize he had left it behind.

The conditions of the course are nearly as pristine as the service. There is a great collection of doglegs and holes with hidden greens that are set up perfectly. You'll need to go over water on some of the holes, avoid large traps on others and stay out of the trees on a few more but the fairways are relatively wide leaving you lots of room to land your drive. The par 3s are relatively short including the 120-yard fifth hole which is easily parable. The back nine starts with a relatively easy par 5 but seems to be a bit more difficult than the front.

As you finish the front nine, take advantage of the walkie-talkie in the mailbox to "call in" your food order for the turn. It's pretty slick and a nice amenity that keeps play moving. Whether you go pizza or hot dog, it's great food and the service in the clubhouse and on the course is top notch.

Eagle Valley does a great job of marking distances on the course. You'll rarely have to walk far to find your yardage as they have put distances on all sprinkler heads and also have regular yardage markers on every hole.

We think Eagle Valley is a gem, combining a beautiful layout with leniency for the ever occasional erratic shot. They package service and amenities at a great price point that leaves golfers wanting to return for another round.

We stopped the white-haired, yet spry, ranger as we were leaving and told him how much he meant to our golfing experience. Then we asked him to keep it up for another 40 years so we can have his job when we're ready to retire.

EMERALD GREENS
(Bronze/Gold)

14425 Goodwin Avenue
Hastings, MN 55033
Clubhouse: 651-480-8558
Golf Shop: 651-480-8558
Type: Public   Par: 72/72

www.emeraldgreensgolf.com

Tees	Men's	Women's	Yards
Red		71.4/118	5493
Gold	67.6/114	72.6/120	5704
White	70.6/119	76.3/129	6361
Blue	71.6/122		6585

Distances specific to this hole combination only.

Course Rating

HOSPITALITY	9.04
PLAYABILITY	7.68
USABILITY	8.71
FACILITY	6.58
VALUE	7.15

OVERALL SCORE
801

Greens Fee: $51.00 (weekend)
1/2 Cart Fee: $15.00 (weekend)

Emerald Greens is a 36-hole complex located in Hastings, Minnesota. It is a large facility with four different 9-hole courses all on one property. They have a good sized practice range, two putting greens with one having a practice bunker, grill service, full bar, cart service, and banquet room. And during the busy season they have a "grill shack" at the turn to get a decent hamburger.

Pulling up to the clubhouse during the summer, do not be swayed by the sheer volume of cars parked on the lot. Emerald Greens takes pride in its ability to host tournaments AND have daily fee golf all in the same day. The Bronze/Gold combination is 6361 yards with a rating of 70.6 and slope 119. The Bronze course is the weakest of the four courses and it shows. While the overall conditions of the course is on par with the other three as it pertains to fairways and greens, it just seems like this nine does not get as much maintenance attention as the others and the layout is slightly haphazard.

They have a lot of signage and it's needed since you often cross by other holes on your way to your next hole. The only lack of signage was on the Bronze course. Cart paths could have been in better shape, most being a gravel path and on occasion they were rutty.

Sand traps were generally raked but the edges looked ratty and in need of some grooming. The quality of the sand was grainy and of the typical "playground" type of grainy sand we find on Minnesota courses. This course is playable and you rarely get in too much trouble with errant shots. It's a little harder in the summer since they let some of the wild grasses grow tall that are between adjacent holes and hitting out of or finding your errant ball is more difficult.

Carts are older and are of the gas type. They really need to get some newer electric carts with GPS, but we can understand their hesitation since they have a fairly large fleet of carts. Yardage markers are plainly marked at 200, 150 and 100 yards. Overall impression is that it is a large course with a multitude of different combination of nines to choose from. For typical golfers it is playable and scoreable.

SOUTHEAST

EMERALD GREENS
(Silver/Platinum)

14425 Goodwin Avenue
Hastings, MN 55033
Clubhouse: 651-480-8558
Golf Shop: 651-480-8558
Type: Public   Par: 72/72

www.emeraldgreensgolf.com

Tees	Men's	Women's	Yards
Red		73.2/128	5789
Gold	70.4/126	76.2/134	6326
White	72.5/130	78.8/139	6792
Blue	74.2/133		7163

Distances specific to this hole combination only.

Region: Twin Cities

Course Rating

HOSPITALITY	8.05
PLAYABILITY	8.01
USABILITY	8.94
FACILITY	7.13
VALUE	7.01

U

OVERALL SCORE
797

Greens Fee: $51.00 (weekend)
1/2 Cart Fee: $15.00 (weekend)

Emerald Greens is found at the corner of Highways 55 and 42 in Hastings, Minnesota. It has four 9-hole courses, a great practice area and a plain but very functional clubhouse. The clubhouse has a small snack area where you can get a hot dog, bratwurst, hamburgers, and soup. Downstairs there are banquet facilities to accommodate 175 people.

The four courses are the Bronze, Silver, Gold, and Platinum. A majority of the time the 18-hole configuration is Bronze/Gold and Silver/Platinum. On this day we played the gold tees on the Silver/Platinum courses.

Overall the whole course is in excellent condition. The owners have done a tremendous amount of work planting trees, landscaping, building beautiful stone bridges, and building elevated tees with large boulders. The tees, fairways, short rough, and greens are well maintained. We were disappointed in the bunkers. They contained playground sand and a large number of them had footprints of players who had failed to rake when leaving. The cart paths are only around the tees and greens. They consisted of badly deteriorated blacktop and gravel, but were functional. Getting from greens to tees was well defined.

Both these nines are relatively flat and easy to walk with the Platinum having a couple of small hills. Being relatively an open course makes it difficult to play in wind, but in the fall it is a good place to play as there are few leaves. They have planted many small trees that will completely change the nature of the course in a few years. The Silver course has a par 3 with a very nice elevated tee to an island green. The Platinum course has a par 5 dogleg that plays 536 yards from the gold tees and 632 yards from the blue tees—very difficult even downwind.

We played on a cool windy day and managed to get around in less than four hours and had little trouble with sprayed shots. We thought that the Silver/Platinum combination played a little long for the higher handicap player. Golfers may find a combination of the other courses to be more enjoyable but challenging due to the shorter lengths.

FOUNTAIN VALLEY

2830 220th Street West
Farmington, MN 55024
Clubhouse: 651-463-2121
Golf Shop: 651-463-2121
Type: Semi-Private   Par: 72
no website

Tees	Men's	Women's	Yards
Red		73.7/127	5797
White	70.7/128	76.6/133	6318
Blue	71.9/130		6560

Region: Twin Cities

Course Rating

HOSPITALITY	7.28
PLAYABILITY	5.94
USABILITY	6.81
FACILITY	5.72
VALUE	6.34

OVERALL SCORE
646

Greens Fee: $29.00 (weekend)
1/2 Cart Fee: $15.00 (weekend)

Golfers tend to categorize golf courses based on their reputation, type or location. Fountain Valley Golf Course, just south of the Twin Cities in Farmington, Minnesota, is a country course. It's not fancy, it's not expensive and it isn't difficult to play. All the basics are there—course, clubhouse, driving range, golf carts—but that is the extent of it.

Carved out of former farm fields, the course is relatively flat with trees that appear to be planted in the last decade so they aren't very large yet. The fairways are wide open with few hazards to speak of until the back nine. Overall condition of the course was average, with tee boxes and fairways holding up well. The putting surface was fast and in excellent condition, but most are billiard table flat with few undulations. Putts roll true so long as you have good aim; they should usually find their destination.

Cart paths, what there are of them, are an afterthought. Distance markers are the standard 200, 150, 100 yards, so you can dial in your distances, but tee box signage is weak, sometimes making the search for the next hole a bit more difficult than necessary.

The facility's layout is compact with a small parking lot just steps from the driving range and clubhouse. A brick patio surrounds the large modern clubhouse and inside is an open area with check-in, a small food counter and a seating area that could accommodate events of at least 150 people. After putting out at the 18th hole, you might consider grabbing a refreshment and bringing it to the patio to watch as other golfers finish up their rounds, but dinner afterwards would have to be found elsewhere.

As a golf experience, this is a no frills, workman-like course. It has all the basics you'd expect, but nothing fancy. Don't expect umbrellas in your mixed drinks or fancy food at the clubhouse. This is a course designed for an easy round of golf that won't stress out you or your wallet. For less skilled players, it is a course that will build confidence. For better players, this is not the track for you.

GOODRICH

1820 North Van Dyke Street
Maplewood, MN 55109
Clubhouse: 651-748-2525
Golf Shop: 651-748-2525
Type: Public   Par: 70

www.ramseycountygolf.com

Tees	Men's	Women's	Yards
Red	64.9/111	69.9/119	5125
White	68.4/118		5914
Blue	69.9/121		6235

Region: Twin Cities

Course Rating

HOSPITALITY	8.42
PLAYABILITY	7.49
USABILITY	8.31
FACILITY	7.11
VALUE	6.72

OVERALL SCORE
775

Greens Fee: $26.00 (weekend)
1/2 Cart Fee: $17.00 (weekend)

Much could be said about a golf course that has the words "good" and "rich" in its name. The good news is that you need to be neither good nor rich to enjoy a round at this hacker-friendly course on the east side of St. Paul. In fact, Goodrich Golf Course is one of the most accessible and playable of the golf courses owned and operated by Ramsey County.

The signature element of Goodrich Golf Course is its indoor golf dome. This multi-level golf facility is open year-round to hone your stroke before a round and to keep sharp in the cold months when golf is nothing more than a distant memory or the product of winter dreams. The course also offers such amenities as outdoor putting and chipping greens, a small patio, on-course beverage service and a pro shop with golf equipment and a small menu of food and beverages. Lessons are available for the novice and the avid golfer alike, and, at under $30 per round, the value is unmistakable.

Although Goodrich is an enjoyable and playable course, it finds itself in tough company. With Keller Golf Course and Manitou Ridge Golf Course (both operated by Ramsey County) within three miles, the seasoned golfer may prefer to play the more extravagant and challenging courses. However, Goodrich is not without its own charm. The course is rarely busy, which makes tee times readily available and the pace of play steady and fast. Because it is not as difficult as other local courses, Goodrich is a good place for the novice golfer to learn the game. The 6200-yard course provides fairways ranging from 140 yards in length to 475 yards. With mature tree lines, the copious pines are the primary hazards, although sand traps are scattered along the fairways with the occasional water trap.

Goodrich is a fairly navigable golf course and has water stations every four holes. Its attendants know the course well, although their customer service leaves some-thing to be desired. In sum, Goodrich is a great course for the novice golfer and a nice place to play for a quick and uninterrupted round. And don't forget the indoor golf dome for those harsh winter months!

HIDDEN GREENS

12977 200th Street East
Hastings, MN 55033
Clubhouse: 651-437-3085
Golf Shop: 651-437-3085
Type: Public   Par: 72
www.hiddengreensgolf.com

Tees	Men's	Women's	Yards
Red		71.3/124	5379
White	68.9/121	74.5/131	5954
Blue	70.4/124		6289

Region: Twin Cities

Course Rating

HOSPITALITY	8.30
PLAYABILITY	5.79
USABILITY	7.97
FACILITY	7.56
VALUE	7.03

OVERALL SCORE
724

Greens Fee: $27.00 (weekend)
1/2 Cart Fee: $14.00 (weekend)

Hidden Greens is located just a few minutes south of Hastings, Minnesota, just off Highway 61. Keep your eyes open for their sign on the left about 4 miles south of town. We found the staff we encountered to be friendly and informative. There is a small clubhouse with some basic necessities, and limited menu selections. On weekends they grill burgers and dogs.

They have a grass driving range, and practice green adjacent to the clubhouse and a short distance from the first tee. Carts are available, although this course would be very walkable. If you like trees, this is the course for you! On nearly every hole, trees can become a scoring/playing factor. This course was cut out of the woods and there is no escaping the abundance of trees and their wrath. On this fall day, the downed leaves were a definite factor, too.

We found that the course length, at just under 6000 yards from the white tees, made the greens very reachable overall in regulation. The fairways are not impossibly narrow, but make no mistake: you will pay with strokes if you are not accurate with your drives and second shots.

On the front nine, the fairways seemed to be a bit tighter than the backside. When we did reach the greens we found them to be in excellent condition and quite playable. For the average golfer, the greens were good sized. There are only four or five bunkers on the entire course, and water comes into play on a couple holes, but is easily avoidable.

Because of all the trees, playing this course at other times during the year without falling leaves would have been a better time. Don't get us wrong though, we liked the course and again the greens were as good as we have played in the area and we found it hacker friendly as far as length and playability from the fairways. If you hit straight and relatively short, you should have a great time. If not….bring a few extra balls and be ready to give several strokes away when hitting back to the fairway from among the leaves and trees.

SOUTHEAST

HIGHLAND NATIONAL

1403 Montreal Avenue
St. Paul, MN 55116
Clubhouse: 651-695-3774
Golf Shop: 651-695-3719
Type: Public   Par: 72
www.golfstpaul.org

Tees	Men's	Women's	Yards
Red		69.8/121	5125
Blue	68.7/124	73.8/130	5843
White	70.3/128	75.7/134	6196
Black	72.4/131		6638

Course Rating

HOSPITALITY	8.05
PLAYABILITY	6.62
USABILITY	6.93
FACILITY	6.34
VALUE	6.35

OVERALL SCORE
697

Greens Fee: $33.00 (weekend)
1/2 Cart Fee: $15.00 (weekend)

Reopened in 2005 after a $4.3 million facelift, Highland National Golf Course has been a fixture in St. Paul, Minnesota, since 1919, and since it has been around for so many years, it seems a bit neglected and in need of another facelift.

The clubhouse is of a Moorish design with a tiled roof and brick walls, and is starting to look its age. The men's bathrooms are actually down a flight of steep stairs, making it not very accessible, especially for those of us with bad knees. Inside it is just one big room with a fifties-era lunch counter that serves an inexpensive breakfast as well as typical golf course food.

This truly is a hacker's course with wide open fairways, ample greens that roll fast and true, and few hazards that will swallow your golf ball. Water is only a factor on the back nine, and the rough, regardless of where it is on the course, is friendly enough that you can usually find your ball again.

Like all busy urban courses, the staff is efficient, but a bit standoffish. There was no starter or public address system telling you who is next up on #1 or a marshal to rush you along if you are lagging, so you'll have to act like you've been to Highland before because no one is going to hold your hand.

The on-course signage is actually quite good for a popular urban course and finding your way along the cart paths is generally pretty intuitive. The golf course has historically had problems with drainage and if it rained recently, remember to wear the right shoes because water sticks around longer than average. The tee boxes and fairways are well maintained, the rough is not at all unruly, but the greens, although large, seemed a bit pockmarked causing a smartly struck putt to sometimes go a bit off line.

On-course, Highland National does most of the little things right with enough bathroom stops, benches and ball washers. It is just a bit tired and overworked. It could use a facelift and the City of St. Paul appears to recognize some of its issues and is currently renovating the #1 and #10 tee boxes and the main putting green.

SOUTHEAST

100

INVER WOOD

1850 70th Street East
Inver Grove Heights, MN 55077
Clubhouse: 651-457-3667
Golf Shop: 651-457-3667
Type: Public   Par: 72
www.inverwood.org

Course Rating

HOSPITALITY	8.42
PLAYABILITY	7.89
USABILITY	7.40
FACILITY	8.28
VALUE	6.14

Tees	Men's	Women's	Yards
Red		71.0/126	5175
Gold	69.0/125	74.4/134	5795
White	70.8/130		6194
Blue	73.2/144		6724

OVERALL SCORE
780

Greens Fee: $36.00 (weekend)
1/2 Cart Fee: $17.00 (weekend)

The moment that you pull into the Inver Wood Golf Course, you know you're at a course that does things in a big way. From the large parking lot, the huge driving range to the broad fairways, this is a course that means business.

The modern clubhouse facility is alongside one of the biggest driving ranges in the Twin Cities. This range may be a bit more expensive for a bucket, but it goes well beyond just a couple of distance targets, with mock fairways and sand traps to hone your shots. Inside the clubhouse is a nice sandwich grill which goes beyond the typical golf course fare.

When you hit the course, you'd better be ready for a workout because it is very hilly and not very walkable. In addition to being an aerobic workout, it also has a 144 slope which is a testament to both the elevation changes as well as the difficulty. If you take a cart you will never lose your way because the paths are well designed and as long as you stay on them, you'll find the next hole. Another great feature are the distance markers. Markers are embedded in the course every 25 yards from 200 yards in so you will always know what club to pull from your bag.

Overall, this course is well tended, intimidating, long and deceptively hard. It is not for the faint of heart. Although the fairways are large and wide, if you can't keep your drives straight, you will find numerous ways to lose golf balls with tree-lined fairway edges and many areas of deep rough. Also, even after a good shot, don't think that you are completely safe because the course offers a number of strategically placed sand bunkers just waiting to swallow your golf ball.

Inver Wood Golf Course may be a bit more expensive than other local courses, but if you are looking for a real golfing challenge at a high quality facility, it's worth the extra cost.

SOUTHEAST

KELLER

2166 Maplewood Drive
St. Paul, MN 55109
Clubhouse: 651-766-4176
Golf Shop: 651-766-4170
Type: Public   Par: 72

www.ramseycountygolf.com

Tees	Men's	Women's	Yards
Red	66.4/119	71.5/129	5373
White	69.4/125	75.2/136	6041
White/Blue	69.8/129		6160
Blue	71.5/132		6566

Region: Twin Cities

Course Rating

HOSPITALITY   7.38
PLAYABILITY   7.50
USABILITY   6.84
FACILITY   6.48
VALUE   5.80

OVERALL SCORE
702

Greens Fee: $34.00 (weekend)
1/2 Cart Fee: $13.00 (weekend)

Stepping onto Keller Golf Course is like stepping back into time when the course was a regular on the PGA Tour and golf luminaries like Ken Venturi and Sam Snead were winning the annual St. Paul Open. No longer a stop on the PGA Tour because at 6566 yards it has become obsolete, it still is a stiff test for regular golfers.

Although it's been forty years since a professional golf event has been played here, Keller still has the feel of a private course with walls lined with awards, photos and tournament history. Golfers check in at the small pro shop and pick up their golf cart from a very friendly "cartman." Like in decades past, your name is called when your group is scheduled to tee off on #1, just steps away.

As soon as you hit your first drive, you will know you are on a course that is different than any other in the area, with tight doglegs, narrow fairways, elevated greens and par 3s that will test your nerve. This reviewer played the course from the blue tees, but most hackers should really consider playing from the 6041-yard white tees because it plays much longer than on paper and course knowledge will really help your score.

The course is well tended, the greens are fast and the cart service is frequent. What isn't up to par, especially for those playing the course for the first time, is the signage, yardage markers and the scorecard. As you step onto each tee box, a sign does show the distances, but finding yardage markers in the fairways is often a challenge. Also, the hole flags don't specify pin placement. Some holes only show one yardage marker thus making club selection more of a guess than should be necessary.

Keller is an Audubon-certified course with bluebird houses and restoration areas acting as out-of-bounds hazards. If you like to walk, you might want to think twice because it is quite hilly, especially the back nine. Another thing that holds this course back is its reputation for slow play, so playing during off times is a safer bet to avoiding those long rounds.

SOUTHEAST

102

LES BOLSTAD

University of Minnesota
2275 West Larpenteur Avenue
St. Paul, MN 55113
Clubhouse: 612-627-4004
Golf Shop: 612-627-4000
Type: Public   Par: 71
www.uofmgolf.com

Tees	Men's	Women's	Yards
Gold	66.6/115	71.8/122	5478
White	69.5/121	75.3/129	6117
Maroon	70.2/123	76.2/131	6278

Region: Twin Cities

Course Rating

HOSPITALITY   7.85
PLAYABILITY   7.00
USABILITY   7.70
FACILITY   5.98
VALUE   6.63

OVERALL SCORE
716

Greens Fee: $35.00 (weekend)
1/2 Cart Fee: $16.00 (weekend)

The Les Bolstad Golf Course, located in St. Paul, Minnesota, is couched in history. This is where local Minnesota golf luminaries like John Harris and Tom Lehman learned their craft and is the site of a dozen men's and women's Big Ten Championships.

The clubhouse feels very much like a fraternity. Old trophies, wall plaques, and signed prints line the walls. The furniture is old and worn out. The kitchen area and bathrooms are in need of a renovation. Maintenance has been deferred and unfortunately, it can been seen on the course as well.

The course when this reviewer visited in the fall appeared to be in tough shape and the holes were very spotty with some being nicely groomed and others not so well. The fairways seemed very hard with large areas of poor grass. Some greens had dead areas while most were very hard as well. Strangely, almost all of the greens slope uphill so a player can hit similar approach shots to most greens. The cart paths were also very inconsistent going from asphalt to gravel to nothing in places.

One oddity of the course is that #10 and #11 actually are the only two holes that are located on the the south side of Larpenteur Avenue. You reach these holes by taking a tunnel under the road. Near and around the clubhouse there are nice plantings, but the layout of the facility seems a bit inefficient with the parking lot in between #9 and #18, but the driving range and #1 located at opposite ends of the course. A bit of walking will be necessary if you are going to hit the driving range first, but the remainder of the course is reasonably compact so a cart isn't necessary.

For golfers affiliated with the University of Minnesota, the pricing is quite reasonable, but for the rest of us, the fees are a bit expensive for what you are getting. It might be exciting to play the same course as some of the greats that graduated from the University of Minnesota, but the course itself isn't that outstanding and only provides limited challenge.

SOUTHEAST

MISSISSIPPI DUNES

Region: Twin Cities

10351 Grey Cloud Trail
Cottage Grove, MN 55016
Clubhouse: 651-768-7611
Golf Shop: 651-768-7611
Type: Semi-Private   Par: 72

www.mississippidunes.com

Course Rating

HOSPITALITY   8.37
PLAYABILITY   8.89
USABILITY   8.04
FACILITY   9.15
VALUE   6.56

P
F

OVERALL SCORE
840

Tees	Men's	Women's	Yards
Gold			5348
White	70.2/138	75.4/135	6009
Member	71.8/141		6343
Blue	72.6/143		6509

Greens Fee: $44.00 (weekend)
1/2 Cart Fee: $16.00 (weekend)

We have all seen the British Open, watched the knee-length prairie grass whipping in the breeze and wondered what it feels like to peer over the edge of a six-foot deep pothole bunker in search of the pin. Alas, links golf is a rare thing in Minnesota. But it is available in Cottage Grove at Mississippi Dunes Golf Course.

This course is not for the faint of heart nor is it for the novice golfer.   Links golf is as difficult as it appears. The bunkers are deep. The rough grass is long. And the fairways are narrow. The course is punishing for those who have difficulty maintaining a straight drive. With its sharp doglegged fairways and blind tee boxes, this course can give anxious fits to even those who can hit it "long and strong" from the tee. For those who can handle the difficult landscape, the humbling hazards at every turn and the inevitable frustrations, this beautiful course is worth the somewhat costly greens fees.

Like most championship courses, the on-course challenges are not the only frustrations. Although the service is impeccable and the snack-and-beverage cart comes around often, the only available beverages on the course are those you pay for. The course is bereft of water stations. Thus, if you are going to invest in a spectacular round of golf, factor in the cost of beverages in addition to the greens fees.

Mississippi Dunes is a well managed golf course. The fairways are immaculate, with multiple cuts of grass and smooth, quick greens. The course is nicely contoured with subtle rolling hills and pitched greens. The many sand hazards are well kept with soft sand and steep edges. Like most links courses, water does not pose much of a hazard, but the sprawling Mississippi River provides scenic views along a number of holes.

This is not the place for a new golfer, nor is it the place for a relaxing round for a hacker. However, for the hacker who seeks adventure and longs to test his game against a rare and difficult golf experience, Mississippi Dunes is worth the while … knickers and kilts are optional.

SOUTHEAST

OAK MARSH

526 Inwood Avenue North
Oakdale, MN 55128
Clubhouse: 651-730-8886
Golf Shop: 651-730-8886
Type: Public   Par: 70

www.wpgolf.com

Tees	Men's	Women's	Yards
Red		66.9/112	4648
Gold	65.9/112	70.4/119	5273
White	68.2/117	73.3/125	5793
Blue	70.0/121		6184

Region: Twin Cities

Course Rating

HOSPITALITY	7.95
PLAYABILITY	7.78
USABILITY	7.19
FACILITY	7.47
VALUE	5.70

OVERALL SCORE
745

Greens Fee: $36.00 (weekend)
1/2 Cart Fee: $16.00 (weekend)

Located in Oakdale, Minnesota, Oak Marsh Golf Course is a compact course that seems out of place surrounded by residential on one side and commercial offices and retail on the other. Like urban courses (this one is actually in a suburb), it must contend with the hubbub and noise of the city, but once you move into the course a few holes, those concerns fade away.

At only 5793 yards from the white tees, you'd think the course provides no challenge. Well, don't prejudge it. Yes, there are some long holes with little by way of hazards, but there are also a number of holes that require hitting over or alongside water. These require you to be judicious when pulling out your driver. Regardless, unless you have a water phobia, the course plays reasonably easy for a hacker.

Where the course seems to slip is the sometimes confusing signage for a first timer and the occasional long distances between holes and from the clubhouse to the first tee. It doesn't have much elevation so walking the course is a definite possibility. It also has a centrally located driving range and putting green very close to the first tee so practicing before your round is very convenient. If you choose a cart, they are equipped with new UpLink GPS, which is a nice feature, but the screen is so large that it requires looking through the windshield from the side.

The clubhouse doubles as an event center and has a full bar, a full-service Oak Marsh Grille, a deck and expansive patio. The course management really emphasizes its function space for weddings and other events and can host up to 300 people. You might get the sense that golf is secondary to events and from a profitability sense, you'd probably be right.

For folks on the east side of the Twin Cities, Oak Marsh Golf Course should be considered as a playing option, but it does tend to be a bit more spendy than similar city courses.

PARKVIEW Exec. 18

1310 Cliff Road
Eagan, MN 55123
Clubhouse: 651-452-5098
Golf Shop: 651-452-5098
Type: Public   Par: 63

www.parkviewgolfclub.com

Tees	Men's	Women's	Yards
Blue		62.8/99	4064
Gold	61.5/98	65.1/104	4479

Region: Twin Cities

Course Rating

HOSPITALITY	7.55
PLAYABILITY	6.33
USABILITY	7.81
FACILITY	5.91
VALUE	5.96

OVERALL SCORE
683

Greens Fee: $27.25 (weekend)
1/2 Cart Fee: $11.75 (weekend)

Known for its "first to open, last to close" policy, Parkview Golf Club is a beginner's course and makes an effort to reach out to juniors and less skilled players. At only 4479 yards from the gold tees, it presents little challenge to accomplished players, but is a good place to learn the ropes.

The course is well used and shows it. When visited, the tee boxes showed a lot of divots and the greens had a number of areas that needed seeding or better maintenance. The course itself is very unimaginative—a lot of flat, straight fairways. Only a few holes present any challenge and you'll find those at the end of your round. For golfers just starting out, be warned that many greens are elevated so even if an approach shot lands on the green, it is likely to roll off the other side, adding to your score.

This is a walker's course and a cart is superfluous and an unnecessary expense. The signage around the course tends to be spotty. Most holes are easy to figure out, but for first timers, the course needs more directional signage and distance markers to make playing easier.

The practice facilities are small, need better maintenance and are not in great shape. The putting green is small and the coin-operated driving range is narrow with odd target hills complete with fake sand traps. A second putting area actually has a couple of practice sand traps that you rarely find at courses around town. They take pace-of-play seriously so watch for the electric chair near the entrance for those who are found to have been convicted of "slow play."

Parkview is a basic, no-frills course. It does try to reach out to the beginner with individual and group lessons as well as golf camps throughout the summer and is a nice place for seniors looking to finish eighteen holes in under 3 ½ hours.

For more accomplished players, this is not the course for you, but for those wanting to work on your game in a relaxed, no-pressure environment, Parkview might be a stop on your itinerary.

SOUTHEAST

PHALEN PARK

1615 Phalen Drive
St. Paul, MN 55106
Clubhouse: 651-778-0424
Golf Shop: 651-778-0413
Type: Public   Par: 70
www.golfstpaul.org

Tees	Men's	Women's	Yards
Red		69.6/116	5311
White	67.5/116		5881
Blue	68.4/118		6092

Course Rating

HOSPITALITY	7.84
PLAYABILITY	6.71
USABILITY	6.86
FACILITY	6.03
VALUE	6.31

OVERALL SCORE
688

Greens Fee: $30.00 (weekend)
1/2 Cart Fee: $14.00 (weekend)

Phalen Park Golf Course is a classic Saint Paul, Minnesota, municipal course mixing a challenging collection of holes with enjoyable service. If you need a little warm-up time upon your arrival there is a decent-sized range and a basic practice green to hone your putting stroke. Their practice area is far from mesmerizing but it does the trick to get the kinks out.

The clubhouse feels more like a rec center but this is a city municipal course so a plush clubhouse should never be expected. The concession stand has all of the things you would expect at a golf course concession stand and also has some of the best hot dogs in the Metro area.

While the course is loaded with trees lining both sides of just about every hole, the holes lay out very nicely for the hacker. The front opens with an easy and relatively short par 4 that is easily parable. The front nine is considerably easier than the back as several blind tee shots come into play.

Because it is a municipal track, the greens and fairways are a bit tattered due to the sheer traffic the course endures. And a lot of that traffic is being pretty rough on the course, evidenced by deep unreplaced divots in the fairways and ball marks on the greens.

If you can get past the blemishes there really are some nice holes including a challenging par 5 on #4. We also liked the par-3 #17 that looks like you have to go over water to get there but the water is actually not in play—if you can convince yourself of that before the shot.

The service overall was welcoming as people in the pro shop, concession stand and on the beverage cart were all extremely friendly.

This course is shorter, playing only a shade over 5800 yards from the middle tees, but don't confuse short with easy. The course will challenge you and you are almost guaranteed to score better after at least one round of experience on it.

SOUTHEAST

PRESTWICK

9555 Wedgewood Drive
Woodbury, MN 55125
Clubhouse: 651-731-4779
Golf Shop: 651-731-4779
Type: Public   Par: 72

www.prestwick.com

Tees	Men's	Women's	Yards
Red		71.2/121	5228
Gold	68.7/120	74.0/127	5740
White	71.3/125	77.2/134	6319
Blue	73.2/130		6750

Region: Twin Cities

Course Rating

HOSPITALITY	7.71
PLAYABILITY	8.84
USABILITY	7.85
FACILITY	7.72
VALUE	5.02

P

OVERALL SCORE
781

Greens Fee: $69.00 (weekend)
1/2 Cart Fee: $17.00 (weekend)

Getting to Prestwick Golf Course, located in Woodbury, Minnesota, was a challenge because the street signage is a bit confusing with Wedgewood on one side of the street and Edgewood on the other. Checking in was a bit off-putting. The person behind the desk seemed like she was having a phone texting emergency and was preoccupied with what was on her cell phone instead of helping us pay and get started. After a few direct questions, she finally realized we had never played there before and then directed her full attention to helping us get going.

We had to wait a bit at the first tee so we chatted up the starter. He was friendly, gave a lot of info about the course, but seemed a bit guarded. When we started to get caught up with the group ahead, they seemed a bit standoffish and paid us no notice. In contrast, the best person of the day was a single golfer. He had a home nearby and Prestwick was his home course. He was warm and welcoming.

The carts are one of the best things about the round. Very nice, clean, newer electric carts with GPS. Second best thing about the round is that you are able to order your turn meal from the cart. Which we did. We even got a confirmation that the order was received. Pretty tasty chicken salad wrap with good kettle chips.

The course itself was in good condition with your usual divots on the par 3s. The fairways were also in good condition and of decent width with an out-of-bounds on almost every hole. When we played the course, if we found ourselves in the sand, it seemed to be of poorer quality and still had not dried up from rain two days previous. The greens were fast and did not hold approach shots as well as anticipated.

The 19th hole, called Axel's at Prestwick, is a full bar and restaurant and does a good business catering to non-golfing customers in the evenings. It has a fireplace, a wall of windows and live music. If our perceptions were only based on the single that joined us, we would think differently about Prestwick. But all other things considered, Prestwick seemed like a semi-private course trying to be private and only put up with non-members because they needed the income.

SOUTHEAST

RICH VALLEY

3855 145th Street East
Rosemount, MN 55068
Clubhouse: 651-437-4653
Golf Shop: 651-437-4653
Type: Public   Par: 64

www.rich-valley-golf-course.com

Tees	Men's	Women's	Yards
Red/White	63.7/95	65.1/99	4924
Red/Blue	64.1/100	64.4/101	5058
White/Blue	63.0/98	63.7/98	5289

Course Rating

HOSPITALITY	7.68
PLAYABILITY	6.18
USABILITY	6.93
FACILITY	6.07
VALUE	6.80

OVERALL SCORE
675

Greens Fee: $25.00 (weekend)
1/2 Cart Fee: $12.00 (weekend)

On your way south on Highway 52 to Rochester, Red Wing and environs, you may find yourself yearning for a little golf as you pass through Rosemount, Minnesota. There you may want to stop in at Rich Valley Golf Club. This 27-hole course is carved out of a former farm field and is still surrounded by corn and soybeans.

Unlike other courses in the area, it does things differently. It is very short with each set of nine holes only about 2500 yards. You can select any two of the nines if you are playing 18 holes and then stop back into the clubhouse to play the remaining nine. The facility has a cozy clubhouse that looks a lot like a large residential house, complete with the owner's catalogs for scrapbooking. The parking lot is a short distance from the front door and the driving range is just around the corner. Inside is a basic layout and food offerings are what you'd typically find.

Although you are really in the country, you can see the skyline of the Rosemount oil refinery in the distance and hear a continual din of highway noise because the course's layout is so open. The course itself is very basic and flat—numerous short par 4s punctuated with an occasional par 5. This is not a course with natural hazards like water or swampy areas so you will be hard-pressed to lose your ball. If you can hit your drives straight, you will feel like a big-time player because you'll be able to drive the green in two.

Getting around the course is easy, but keep checking the map because signage is very poor and hard to see from a distance. Course conditions are average, with an apparent lack of ongoing maintenance. Hole positions seem to not have changed over the summer, sand traps were quite gravelly and hard, and the women's tees look like they were just an afterthought.

As a playing challenge, this is not a very difficult course. If you are there for an interesting round you'll be disappointed. If you want to play a quick round at a local, small-town, inexpensive track that is a good place for beginners, then Rich Valley will work for you.

SOUTHEAST

RIVER OAKS

11099 South Highway 61
Cottage Grove, MN 55016
Clubhouse: 651-438-2121
Golf Shop: 651-438-2121
Type: Public   Par: 71

www.riveroaksmunigolf.com

Region: Twin Cities

Course Rating

HOSPITALITY	9.24
PLAYABILITY	8.95
USABILITY	9.01
FACILITY	8.25
VALUE	6.95

H
P
U

OVERALL SCORE
873

Tees	Men's	Women's	Yards
Red		69.9/120	5165
White	69.2/123		5956
Blue	71.4/127		6418

Greens Fee: $32.50 (weekend)
1/2 Cart Fee: $15.50 (weekend)

Even a novice golfer can appreciate the distinctions that make a well-managed golf course stand out from the rest. The grass seems greener there, the staff friendlier, the greens smoother, the pace of play steadier and the sense of contentment reflected by the patrons is unmistakable.   If these subtleties elude you, defer to the judgment of other golfers by gauging how far in advance you need to book your tee time. Many very nice courses do go unnoticed, but word spreads quickly about the really good courses, which can make booking a tee time your first challenge.

Located off of Highway 61 just south of Cottage Grove, Minnesota, River Oaks is a sprawling 6400-yard course located in the beautiful Mississippi River Valley. Its varied holes present breathtaking, panoramic views of the Mississippi River, mature tree lines and cleverly placed hazards, which can frustrate the ambitious golfer who would prefer to "go for the green" rather than lay up with a more prudent shot. However, that is not to say that River Oaks is designed exclusively for the "scratch" golfer. One of the more enjoyable aspects of this course is that it provides avenues for a variety of shots, forcing the golfer to think through a strategy for attacking the pin.

With its numerous amenities, it is no small wonder why River Oaks is often fully booked with weekend tournaments and events. The inviting clubhouse and veranda provide a relaxing venue to rehash your round or to host an event. More often than not the head golf pro, Bruce Anderson, will welcome you to River Oaks and the starter or ranger will wish you well or stop to ask how you are enjoying your round. Along the course, you will find plenty of water stations and restrooms to make your round more comfortable. In addition, your beer, soda or sports drink will barely be empty by the time the refreshment cart makes its way back to your group. Although you may need to plan ahead to book a tee time, River Oaks is a great place to play one or more rounds over the course of the summer. Even at full price, $32.50 for a weekend round, the value is unmistakable.

SOUTHEAST

SOUTHERN HILLS

18950 Chippendale Avenue West
Farmington, MN 55024
Clubhouse: 651-463-4653
Golf Shop: 651-463-4653
Type: Public   Par: 71
www.southernhillsgolfcourse.com

Course Rating

HOSPITALITY	8.31
PLAYABILITY	7.19
USABILITY	8.12
FACILITY	7.07
VALUE	7.39

V

Tees	Men's	Women's	Yards
Red		68.1/118	4970
White	69.1/125	74.2/131	6073
Blue	70.1/128		6314

OVERALL SCORE
766

Greens Fee: $36.25 (weekend)
1/2 Cart Fee: $14.75 (weekend)

Southern Hills Golf Course in Farmington, Minnesota, provides a good balance of playability, interesting hole layouts, and good course conditions.

The clubhouse is a very unique structure with a porch that wraps around all four sides and a dining hall. It would make for a great place to have a cocktail on a warm summer evening.

The practice area is a long narrow green that was groomed very well. The green allowed any practice putt you could imagine from big breakers to straight tap-ins. The driving range was rather small and located down the left side of the first hole creating a close out-of-bounds area.

Staff was very friendly upon arrival, but on-course staff seemed to be lacking for a Sunday morning. There was no starter or even a call to let you know you were up. Also with the start times being only 8 minutes apart, there is a need for a ranger to be "laying down the law" on the course to keep the pace of play to a reasonable rate.

The course provides enough challenge for the hacker but not too much as to make the experience unenjoyable. While there are not many trees which come into play, it does yield a vast amount of other hazards which are located quite well in landing zones. Many of these hazards could be avoided with a little course knowledge. There is a variety of holes from short par 4s to long par 3s, many of which offer some good risk/reward opportunities. The par 5s are all very reachable but are very strategically protected so "going for it" does not come without some risk.

The overall shape of the course was very good. Fairways were nice and green, but a little shaggy. Greens rolled true and had a good pace but were very puttable. The rough was a little dry, but was all cut to a manageable length except in the hazard areas where it was allowed to grow wild. Navigating the course seemed quite easy except for a couple of adjacent tee boxes and small tee signs.

SOUTHEAST

VALLEYWOOD

4851 125th Street West
Apple Valley, MN 55124
Clubhouse: 952-953-2324
Golf Shop: 952-953-2324
Type: Public   Par: 71

www.cityofapplevalley.org

Tees	Men's	Women's	Yards
Red	65.2/109	69.4/117	4960
Blue	70.0/119	75.3/129	6030
Gold	71.8/122		6407

Region: Twin Cities

Course Rating

HOSPITALITY	6.82
PLAYABILITY	6.36
USABILITY	7.54
FACILITY	6.87
VALUE	5.93

OVERALL SCORE
675

Greens Fee: $53.00 (weekend)
1/2 Cart Fee: $15.00 (weekend)

While there are tougher tests out there than Valleywood Golf Course in Apple Valley, Minnesota, it combines just enough length with the demand for precise shot-making in such a way to make it better suited for separating a flight of low-handicap golfers in a white-knuckle tournament format than for a casual round with the guys on a Sunday afternoon.

The course was in terrific shape. The fairways were green and trimmed and dotted by only the expected number of healing divots, and the rough was nice and green yet short enough to play from with a fairway wood most of the time. The greens were a little firmer than expected given recent rain, but most still held an iron shot even if it wasn't perfectly struck. Many of them were domed or undulating, however, making chips and long putts a bit of an adventure. Pace of play was on the slow side but that might have been because it was Father's Day and there were a couple of families taking Dad out for a round that weren't familiar with the etiquette of the game. The rangers did a nice job of minimizing the impact on the rest of the players.

The on-course amenities were merely adequate. The beverage cart stopped by every four or five holes and the staff was friendly and accommodating. The selections were the usual golf course fare—beer and soft drinks on the cart, hot dogs and brats at the concessions stand in the clubhouse—and the prices were reasonable. There were no bathrooms on the course, so we had to either use the porta-potties or wait until we reached the clubhouse, which itself was pretty utilitarian (there was, however, a complimentary bottle of sunscreen in the men's room for anyone who'd forgotten theirs, which was a pleasant surprise).

All told, Valleywood is a good choice for the golfer who's looking for an enjoyable yet challenging on-course experience and doesn't much care about anything else, but if you're a 20+ handicap looking for a relaxing round with your buddies followed by dinner and drinks at the 19th hole, you might want to spend your weekend elsewhere.

SOUTHEAST

Buy Our Guide, Help the Environment

The Hacker's Guide is a proud sponsor of Audubon International.

About Audubon International

Since the 1990s, Audubon International has created partnerships with landowners to enhance wildlife habitat and protect water quality. Today more than 2,200 "cooperative sanctuaries" are located throughout the United States, including golf courses, homes, businesses, and entire communities.

Golf has a unique role to play in caring for our environment. By their very nature, golf courses provide significant natural areas that benefit people and wildlife in increasingly urbanized communities across North America. At the same time, golf's use of chemicals, water, and other resources to maintain playing conditions is often criticized for threatening the quality of our environment. The Audubon International's *Golf & the Environment Initiative* seeks to assist golf courses in becoming a valuable part of our conservation landscape, while building support for more eco-friendly golf throughout the golf industry.

The award-winning Audubon Cooperative Sanctuary Program for Golf Courses has designated over 660 golf courses worldwide as Certified Audubon Cooperative Sanctuaries, 23 of which are in Minnesota.

For each *Hacker's Guide* that is purchased, we will donate a portion of our proceeds to Audubon International. By purchasing one of our guides, you are also helping the environment.

For more information, visit **www.golfandenvironment.org** or **www.auduboninternational.org**.